Problems Beget Profits, A Professional Manager's Playbook

Keep your Managerial Skills in Shape

I0468448

Rory Evans Wilson

www.watchforgod.org

Other Books by Rory Evans Wilson:

Farm Life, *Memories of Old and the Gift of New Life*

The Portage, *Mekanayzn Nongo (Path Today)*

The Speakers, *And the Sacred Truth*

Speak To Me Again, *Poems and Reflections - For modern times; for all time*

The Spirit Inside Us, *Reflections and messages concerning faith and life*

Robe of Life, *The Stone and the Lance Lord*

Liberty and Virtue, Freedom and Faith, *Dissertation of the United States of America - its Constitution and Government*

Significant: *The Essence of Our Existence*

Life, A Most Precious Gift

Watch For God

Problems Beget Profits, A Professional Manager's Playbook

Keep your Managerial Skills in Shape

Rory Evans Wilson
Rory Books
www.watchforgod.org

Problems Beget Profits, A Professional Manager's Playbook,
Keep your Managerial Skills in Shape

ISBN- 13: 978-1530857975
ISBN- 10: 153085797X
BISAC: Management/Leadership/Business

Author's Note:

I dedicate this book to the many people who made an extra effort to set me on the right path, guide me in my travels, and provide me insight and knowledge along the way.

Introduction

All successful organizations have come very close to failure at some point in their past. Including the subset of companies that do fail the percentage of entities that encounter potentially fatal situations in the course of their existence is close to 100%. Problems in an organization should therefore be considered normal phenomenon. Just as a baseball team will encounter 24 to 27 outs in a game, getting called "out" in a play does not prevent the team from proceeding with the game. The coach takes each situation as it stands and applies the best strategy possible considering the circumstances to try and win the game. "Outs," like problems, are just a part of the game. How the professional manager deals with a problem and how he/she leverages the situation to drive improvement in the organization is critical to a company's continued existence, growth, and success.

In fact, a company that never has any difficulties and sails along smoothly year after year is also the company that no one ever remembers because they typically stay where they are and do not grow, move, or change and eventually, quietly close their doors when the product or service they provide is no longer needed. In order for a professional manager to drive improvement there must be problems that he/she can turn into profits. All companies have problems so the professional manager, in tune with the need for driving change through improvements in the company, will look for and dig out problems and leverage them to get the organization to a better place.

It is the author's hope that you will identify the problems in your department or organization and apply the basic management principles in this playbook to help you get to a new level. The techniques in this book have been proven to be successful. By embracing and understanding these keys to success you will be in a position to move yourself and your company to a professional level of management and ensure that in the future problems will beget profits.

Contents

You may have one initial hire date and training period but as a professional manager you employ and engage your people every day – you never stop hiring their talents from them and you never stop training them to be better.

Chapter 1 – Assemble a Top-Notch Team

Change has no beginning and no end. It is forever present, seeking to build or erode, destroy or satisfy. It is always present in our earthly environment, in the totality of the human presence, and within each and every one of us. Change is what we fight and avoid, yet at the same time it is what we seek! To harness change and drive change to the betterment of the organization a manager must channel the change occurring in the employees that he/she hires into the workforce – a workforce designed to accomplish change.

With change comes a close relative – problems. Problems result from change, and at the same time drive the need for change. Not knowing for sure what came first, the chicken or the egg, it is not clear whether problems precede and cause change, or if change precedes and causes problems. In many ways both are so interconnected as to sometimes be viewed as one in the same. Problems cannot exist for an organization without people. People are not a requirement for change to exist as the mountains will continue to breakdown from wind, sun, and rain. Simultaneously mountains will push up through the earth's crust as tectonic activity from our magmatic core drives change on the surface of the planet. We are all living on one spinning sphere, ever changing, constantly moving, with or without humans to allegedly preside over it.

People are the sole purpose behind consumption and commerce, trade, business and economy. Without people the need for these activities would not exist. Humans bring problems into the equation as we strive to improve the economy of our existence.

How does all of this relate to hiring people? It is important to understand that all people are constantly going through changes in their lives. The fact that you are looking to hire someone is evidence that your organization is going through a change. You may have lost an employee and are looking to replace them. You may be expanding your workforce and need more people to keep up with the changes occurring in your operation. The applicants you interview are also going through a change. They may have lost their jobs for many different reasons or they may be looking to change what they are doing for personal or professional reasons. All the components of the hiring process are centered on change.

Our aphorism is "problems beget profits." As we recognize that change and problems exist together in the work environment, the approach we use and the level of understanding of this landscape will prepare us to make the most of hiring situations. A professional manager will drive forward their business endeavors leveraging the hiring situation to their organizational advantage. Remember without people there are no problems; without problems there is no need for change; without change there is no impetus for improvement; without improvement there is little opportunity for growth and profit.

Hiring

The single most important management decision you will make is who to hire into your team. Hiring the right person for the right reason; a person who fits the position and provides compatibility as well as diversity of thought among the other team members is critical to your success as a manager. You should try to always hire people who have the ability of performing one level higher than the one you are recruiting them for but be careful not to hire people who think they should be another level up in the organization when they start in their first position. Seeing the future potential in a candidate before it is realized by the person themselves can provide upward bandwidth for you in developing and promoting the growth of the new employee while providing job satisfaction and retention for them as well.

Recruiting

Recruiting can be a difficult task depending upon the current labor market conditions of supply and demand as well as availability of people who have the competencies and experience or training that you are looking for. What seems to be the common-place and standard methods of recruiting can many times be the least productive. Successful methods of finding good people to interview and hire tend to be found in a few key areas:

Steal from the competition or from other industries that are similar. The key point here is that good employees are generally not looking to make a job change and you will rarely find their resume if they even have a current one. It should be noted that intentionally hiring people away from a specific competitor with the intent to cause disruption and damage to the competitor is not an acceptable management practice and could result in legal issues. Remember we are professional managers and work hard to protect that image of ourselves and to do so we abide by professional credos displaying respect and maintaining credibility.

Community involvement and networking with school career counselors, participating in college job fairs, engaging in internship programs, networking with local business organizations and social groups can be a great source. These candidates will tend to have more potential because they are known and referred by people who are willing to endorse them to you. Again, these candidates may otherwise not be looking for a position within your department or company without the suggestion or recommendation from someone they know and trust.

Referrals from customers and other employees can also be a great source and method of connecting a person who may not be looking at your position with a candidate that you may never see on a posting site. In some cases the social aspects of the hiring referral may create an interest in a good employee who is gainfully working and happy in their current position with another company and would not have been looking at your position or any new position without the suggestion from a person in your organization.

One of the best sources of candidates is from internal development. Allocating time to on-going training and development of your existing employees can be the best method of recruiting into future openings. Doing this allows you the ability to shift people from lower graded and entry-level work into more intriguing and interesting work as employees look to move up within the organization. It is much easier to hire people into entry-level positions and develop them over time to the culture and proficiencies required to keep the company or department moving forward. This process takes time and attention and will not work in all situations but staffing a mixture of internally developed people with successful external recruiting will provide a refreshing balance for your team.

The most common and least successful methods of finding good people fall into traditional hiring categories that are all too familiar:

Job service and other placement services fail for many reasons. The most prevalent reason is the motivation to sell an applicant to you. This is driven by the recruiting agencies need to move people through the process to get paid. In some respects, this makes sense as they should only get paid for producing results. The placement of a person that does not fit well into the organization can cost you a lot and you may not realize it until it is too late.

"Help Wanted" advertising and social media get the attention of people who are searching for a change in their current work situation. There are many good people who are stuck in a bad situation and you may be able to recruit them into a job within your organization at which they will do very well. The flipside of this recruiting is the likelihood that the people you recruit are looking to leave a position because they are not good workers or have motivational problems or work behaviors that you do not want.

The old "Sign in the window" type thinking tends to speak to a specific audience only. Typically, this form of recruiting is directed at a subset of people that are looking for a job versus those who are not. People who are gainfully employed and happy in their current positions tend to ignore signs and advertising for jobs in another company.

I will never forget the young person who showed up in the lobby one morning filling out an application to work in the warehouse. He had an easy going and pleasant attitude and you could tell that he had something unique in his personality that made you curious to know more about him. At one point he was laughing and joking with another applicant as he helped her fill out her application. What the details of his work experience penciled onto the paper revealed was a kid who had been working hard labor jobs for years starting at a young age and was currently unemployed. Having a high school diploma but only one year of college, his overall experience was nothing close to what would be considered minimum qualifications for the job. The company took a chance on this person and hired him into a clerical position on a night shift in the warehouse. Twenty-five years later this night clerk was operating in the role of general manager for the entire operation.

The secret to hiring the right person can sometimes come down to simple luck, basic intuition, gut feel, and yes sometimes – taking a chance on someone that might not yet know themselves what they are capable of. I noticed that the human resource person who took this risk also did so in many other situations. I learned and applied some of his techniques successfully hiring and developing people very much like he did with the young person in the story above.

Interviewing

The key to a successful interview is preparation. Always include the right mix of interviewers on your interview team and keep the total at two or three. Always schedule the interviews back-to-back for about 30 to 45 minutes each but keep the interviews to one-on-one sessions. More than one person interviewing a candidate at the same time can cause issues with the communication and listening process as well as distracting or causing undue stress on the interviewee. Include on your interview team management people from your department and of course always yourself as the hiring manager. It is helpful to include someone from another department on the list of interviewers who can give another perspective on the candidate versus the current people on your team and yourself. You may want to include on your interview team people reporting to you or reporting to your peers who are developing in their roles. This can be powerful in several ways: 1) interviewing responsibility will be considered positive by the developing employee that you include in the process, 2) they will become better vested in the hiring decision, 3) they tend to be closer to the actual work and therefore may be at a better level of understanding regarding the work required of the new hire. Because of this they may be able to spot positive or negative traits in the candidate relative to the position for which they are applying.

Once the interview team is set you will need to identify the characteristics and qualifications desired for the position. You should work to achieve consensus with the interview team so they have a sense for what you are looking for in the candidate. You may agree in advance on the questions to ask the candidate so that all of the key areas are covered in the process. You may also ask questions that enable you to gauge the responses across the interview team to rank the candidate in several common areas. Always regard in high esteem the attitude, knowledge, and behavior of the interviewee. Always react in a positive and professional manner as an interviewer. Open and close the interview on a positive note and make sure you are coming across sincere, interested, and confident. Setting up an interview environment that is calm and relaxing will allow the interviewee to be relaxed and provide better responses to your questions. You will learn more, good or bad, about the candidate if you create an open and comfortable environment. Above all else, make sure that you engage in effective listening.

What is meant by effective listening and what benefits are achieved when applied? Effective listening skills are the ability to actively understand information provided by the speaker, and display interest in the topic discussed. It can also include providing the speaker with feedback, such as asking pertinent questions; so the speaker knows the message is being understood. Effective listening is one of the talents that a leader or manager must develop to be successful. Listening skills are also extremely important for an effective exchange of information between two individuals.

Effective listening helps you develop better open-ended questions. Your questions will be less redundant and better understood by the interviewee. Through effective listening you can become more sensitive to the strengths and weaknesses of the interviewee and do a better job of recognizing interests, abilities, and overall potential. Effective listening means looking for feelings and attitudes. It also means listening for facts and opinions. Be alert for silence and hesitations from the interviewee during the discussion. How well does the candidate listen to what you ask them? This may give you an indication of how well they will listen to you if you hire them. You can use effective listening to get a handle on the perception you receive when the interviewee walks into the room as you maintain focus on both verbal and non-verbal cues. Effective listening means providing accurate feedback to the interviewee. If you receive a sufficient answer to a question, be careful not to go on through your list of questions if they become unnecessary. Trust your gut feel and your judgment on what you see in the candidate. Effective listening will help you strengthen your interviewing skills, allow you to have better control over the interview process, be more organized, and ultimately better able to compare applicants and select the person best suited for the position.

In today's world it can be a challenge to know what to ask or what can get you in trouble if you do ask the wrong question in an interview. Mostly it is common sense and responsible behavior that should guide you in the questions you ask an applicant; however, it is always helpful to know the specifics regarding interviewing do's and don'ts. The following list provides guidelines on what can and what cannot be asked in the interview process. It is extremely important that you review the list and make sure that your questions during the interview are permitted. Failure to follow these guidelines represents an unacceptable management practice and can result in legal issues for the company and yourself.

1. During the interview you may ask the interviewee their name; however you may not inquire into any title which indicates race, color, religion, sex, national origin, handicap, age, or ancestry.
2. You may inquire into place and length of current address; however you may not inquire into foreign addresses which would indicate national origin.
3. Any inquiry limited to establishing that applicants meet any minimum age requirement that may be established by law is acceptable; however requiring a birth certificate or baptismal record before hiring or any other inquiry which may reveal whether the applicant is forty (40) years of age or older is not acceptable.
4. None of the following is acceptable: any inquiry into place of birth, any inquiry into place of birth of parents, grandparents or spouse, and any other inquiry into national origin.
5. You cannot ask any question which would indicate race or color.
6. You cannot ask any question which would indicate sex. Furthermore you cannot engage in any inquiry made of members of one sex, but not the other.

7. Any inquiry which would indicate or identify religious denomination or custom is not acceptable. Applicant may not be told any religious identity or preference of the employer. You may not request a pastor's recommendation or reference.

8. As it relates to handicap situations, you are permitted any inquiry necessary to applicant's ability to substantially perform specific job without significant hazard; however you are not permitted any other inquiry which would reveal handicap.

9. It is acceptable to ask whether an applicant is a citizen, and if not, whether applicant intends to become one. You may ask if their residence is legal and then require proof of citizenship after person is hired. You cannot ask if native-born or naturalized or whether parents or spouse are native-born or naturalized. You cannot ask for proof of citizenship before hiring.

10. Photographs may be required after hiring for indemnification purposes; however you cannot require a photograph before hiring.

11. You are permitted inquires into conviction of specific crimes related to qualifications for the job applied for; however you are not permitted any inquiry which would reveal arrests without convictions.

12. You may inquire into nature and extent of academic, professional, or vocational training and ask about language skills, such as reading and writing of foreign languages (if applicable to position). You may not engage in inquiry to reveal the nationality or religious affiliation of a school or inquire as to mother tongue or how foreign language ability was acquired.

13. You can inquire into a relative's name, relationship, and address of person to be notified in case of emergency; however any inquiry about a relative which would be unlawful if made about the applicant cannot be asked.

14. You may inquire into organizations and offices held, excluding any organization, the name or charter of which indicates the race, color, religion, sex, national origin, handicap, age, or ancestry of its members. You are not permitted inquiry into all clubs and organizations where membership is held.

15. It is acceptable to inquire into service in the armed forces when such service is a qualification for the job. You may ask for a required military discharge certificate after the person is hired. You cannot inquire into military service in armed service of any other country or request military service records or inquire into type of discharge.

16. You may ask about willingness to work required schedule; however inquiry into willingness to work any particular religious holiday is not permitted.

17. You may ask questions required to reveal qualifications for the job applied for; however any non-job related inquiry which may reveal information permitting unlawful discrimination cannot be asked.

18. General personal and work references not relating to race, color, religion, sex, national origin, handicap, age, or ancestry can be asked. Request for references specifically from clergyman or any other persons who might reflect race, color, religion, sex, national origin, handicap, age, or ancestry of applicant cannot be asked.

Many times interviewers get too concerned about the details of what an applicant has done and what their technical capabilities are. If you are hiring someone to make sure the wiring is right on the main computer board controlling the next Mars spaceship all of the interview questions should be related to the individuals technical aptitude and experience. Beyond rocket science and other highly technical fields, brain surgery, cancer research, nuclear physics, etc. you should allow a balanced portion of questions around getting to know who the applicant is as a person.

Who you are is important. I have several close friends who have come to live and work in America from other parts of the world. They notice and have mentioned to me that in America we start a conversation by introducing ourselves and what we do, what position or title we have, and what company we work for. To my friends this seems contrary to them as in their world people introduce each other more from the perspective of who they are, what they enjoy, and what they do outside of the work environment.

Does it mean that Americans spend more time working and grade themselves based upon their achievements derived from their employment? Are Americans driven by capitalistic behavior and are therefore more productive? I do not know the answers to these questions but I know that this observation has helped me in the hiring process as I am looking for a balance between what a person has done as well as who the person is. I like to ask about a person's hobbies, explore how they interact socially and what they enjoy doing with their family, community and friends. I sometimes learn more about a person from their interactions with people in general versus the details of their work experience.

Having owned my own business and also having been a part owner of a small corporation I have come to the belief that a company can be built on the product it produces; but more than that a company can be built based on the strengths and abilities of the people it employs. Given a choice, I prefer to build upon the capabilities of the people who comprise the organization and use their strengths to differentiate my business from the competition. In the end it is the people who have the ability and drive to confront issues, fix problems, break things that are not broken to make them better, think and act on changes to the business to keep it alive and healthy in a stressful economic environment; it is all of these attributes that make the key difference. Hiring the right people will beget profits for your organization stemming from the choice you make about them and from their decision to work for you.

Diversity is only a label we use when we fail to look inside each other to see the blessings and values that we possess and how being different and unique makes us all the same.

Chapter 2 – Team Balance

Personality Type Appreciation

There are many tools that you can use to identify personality types within your team and workgroup. Going through the exercise can be helpful to obtain a better grasp of how different people will respond in various situations and also how they will tend to interact with you and with others. Using popular tools to help your team assess where they and their peers are at in the personality matrix will help people have a better appreciation of the strengths and differences that everyone has. It will also help people understand how the team is benefiting from difference versus struggling with difference. A balanced mixture of people and personality types contribute to a more rounded as well as better decision-making process resulting in a more effective workgroup.

Why is this so important? Not everyone is capable of being the best at everything. As a manager you must resist the temptation to discount the ideas of others who are not similar to yourself. You must not allow your team members to ostracize someone who has a different perspective. It is the difference in people's perspectives when brought together in a positive fashion that provides the most innovative and practical solutions for the business. You truly want a complimentary mixture of people on your team.

As a manager you must also resist the temptation to hire people that are like you. Too many people reporting to you who think like you and do not provide a challenge to the status quo or a viewpoint that is different may leave you and your department struggling at some point. To see and adjust to changes in the business environment and identify effective plans to support new business growth you want to have a team that covers the gambit of strengths across the entire personality matrix.

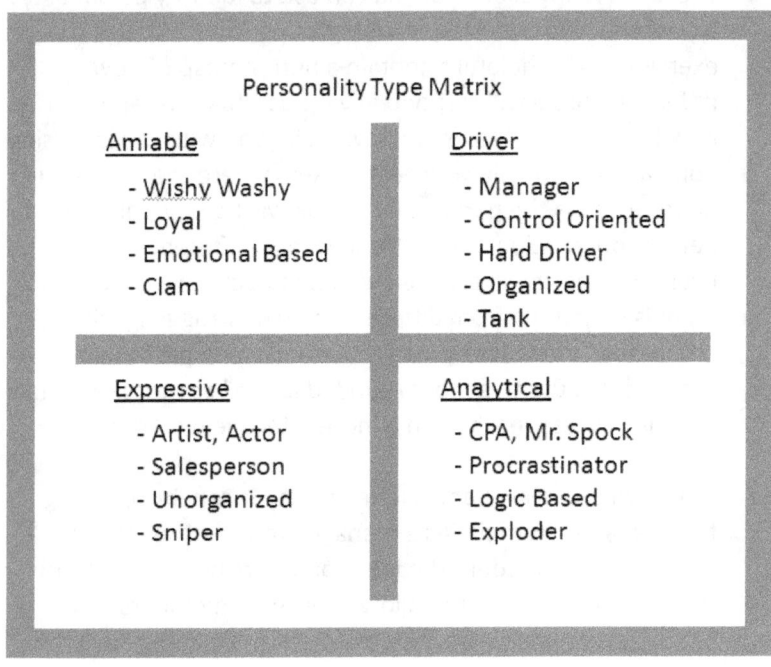

Personality Type Matrix

Amiable
- Wishy Washy
- Loyal
- Emotional Based
- Clam

Driver
- Manager
- Control Oriented
- Hard Driver
- Organized
- Tank

Expressive
- Artist, Actor
- Salesperson
- Unorganized
- Sniper

Analytical
- CPA, Mr. Spock
- Procrastinator
- Logic Based
- Exploder

Amiable and Analytical

Although opposites on the matrix due to the amiable group being emotionally based versus the analytical which is logic based, both of these groups have many things in common.

Both groups are made up of hard-working and dedicated employees that just want people to like them. They also represent the largest percentage of workers in society comprising from 60% to 80% of the average workforce depending upon the industry and business sector. These two groups are also less likely to drive change or cause disruption and will tend to be less inclined to take risks and advance. They tend to maintain employment in a secure and stable location for as long as they can and create a stable base within the workgroup. Always watching the show created by the other two personality types they are prone to support whatever creates the least resistance. Faced with conflict an amiable person will clam up. It will be hard for them to confront conflict. For the analytical person facing conflict, they will put it off as long as possible and then explode. Neither groups embrace conflict.

Expressive

We are all captivated by the expressive. They are the ones on the movie screen, on the radio and TV. The entertainer that we love to watch perform represents a smaller percentage of the workforce. If your department is sales, your team will primarily be made up of expressive people. They have the ability to persuade others in their thinking and because they are not logic-based, will play on people's feeling and emotions to get things done. Having too many expressive people in your workgroup can become a problem so a proper balance is always needed; to be safe approximately 10% to 20%. Expressive people are not always headed in the right direction and can be unorganized and scattered in their work. When faced with conflict they also become non-confrontational and will snipe at management through others. Usually it is the amiable and analytical groups that the expressive people use to get at management while lobbying for support for their position. Management may not even be aware of the sniping that is occurring with their expressive team members. Without the expressive people in the workgroup the organization becomes stagnant as the ability to grow sales, develop new products and markets, and support innovation and creativity in the business generally comes from the expressive group.

Driver

The drivers are the managers. This is the group that tends to drive the business forward. Their logic-based personality helps them to set a clear path while their organizational ability keeps the business on-track. There are fewer people in this group within the workforce, around 10% to 20% approximately. Too many drivers in a workgroup will cause too many disagreements on the direction to take. Also, too many people who may act independently can cause the organization to lose focus. If you have ever been in a setting surrounded by "Type A" personalities, all controlling an event or deciding course of action, it can be a painful experience. You need to make sure you have the right number of bosses on your team and give them well defined space to operate in order to keep from creating conflict. A driver will confront conflict and work to resolution finding that approach to be the most efficient and economical. The driver however will enact decisions and provide direction, assume everyone is at their level of understanding and conviction, continue to march ahead not always knowing whether anyone is following them or not. Communication is an area that a driver should always focus on. They must apply extra effort to hear what the team is saying and make sure everyone is agreeable to the direction the group is heading. This is important to the manager to ensure that the team is following them and headed in the correct direction.

As a manager you need to think through situations from your people's perspective and develop a plan to manage situations and changes in the business. Knowing, or at least being better able to anticipate how a person will react, gives you the opportunity to approach a situation in a more effective manner and will help you to achieve the desired objective.

Remember what is perceived by many as a problem will be viewed by the professional manager as a mechanism to drive improvement and profit in the organization. I worked for a company once that shifted focus at the senior management level from valuing the contribution of people and innovation within the business equation to valuing the financial perspective in a microcosm. The senior leaders became people with financial backgrounds who hired and surrounded themselves with people just like themselves who also had financial backgrounds. Before long the business made structural change decisions and acquisitions that on paper looked good financially but from a business perspective changed the entire culture and representation of the company both internally and externally. Stock prices fell to a fraction of the traditional average for the company. The company had always been regarded as a strong and reliable investment prior to that. Key people with strong business experience who had developed important interpersonal relationships with the employee and customer base left the organization. The company, which was once the most progressive in its industry, fell apart at the seams and continues to struggle for survival today.

Were there other market factors that brought the company down? Sure there were many factors however the senior management team could not turn a problem into a profit because they did not have the team required to accomplish the objective. This chapter is important because the professional manager will see the value in a balanced workgroup and take action to make it better through hiring and developing people properly. The company I referenced did not know or see their failure in time or possibly at all because their focus was somewhere else. As a professional manager you must maintain focus on all aspects of the business at all times. Remember your team is comprised of people, not balance sheets!

A wilderness traveler sets the compass on true North and orients the map so that the party being led stays on course and does not get lost – orient your people well and guide them to their destination.

Chapter 3 – Start Out Right - Orient and Train

Once the initial recruiting and hiring process is complete there are a few critical pieces to take into consideration to achieve successful staffing of your department. Basically there are three distinct aspects of bringing a new employee into the organization:

1. Orientation
2. Advisor/Mentor relationship
3. Training

Orientation helps the employee better understand the purpose of the overall organization; it introduces them to the people and the work that they do to support the team's efforts. The advisor/mentor relationship provides a place for a new employee to open up when there are questions, particularly when they are not sure how things are handled both informally and formally; this relationship helps the new employee integrate into the culture of the organization. Effective orientation and training will provide years of productive results if handled correctly in the beginning.

New Hire Orientation

It is very important that you plan for and follow orientation guidelines and an orientation plan for each new employee. To provide a consistent, welcoming, and comprehensive on-boarding process for new hires a formalized checklist should be used. It is also good to include key people in your department in the orientation process. You should consider assigning an on-boarding advisor to assist with the new hire's transition. While you can serve as the advisor, it is generally recommended that someone in a similar role or at a similar level as the new hire serve as the advisor. The benefits of assigning an advisor will manifest in numerous ways:

> - Reduced workload for you as manager
> - Leadership development opportunity for the advisor
> - Relationship building for new hire with another individual on the team
> - Creates a comfort zone for new hire's simple questions (e.g., where is bathroom)
> - You are not bogged down with all of the orientation tasks and can delegate the simpler tasks of orienting the new hire to someone on your team
> - It makes the new hire feel comfortable and welcome in the new environment

It is important that you establish in advance the meeting schedule for all basic training and orientation that the new hire needs. You need to coordinate the schedule with other people and departments so they are ready and can support you in the process. Make sure that you include ALL departments so the new hire is introduced to the broader team, and not just their own department. It is good to prepare the calendar of meetings and orientation tasks but make it the new hire's responsibility to adjust the schedule as needed and record dates on their copy of the orientation checklist when a task is complete.

How often do you hear the story told about how someone got oriented to their job by getting thrown into the fire on the first day with no training or orientation to the team! As much as you feel like you are struggling and behind because you need to get a position filled, in the long-run you will never get caught up if you do not take the proper time to orient your newly hired employee to the work and workgroup. As a professional manager you must embrace all the components of the orientation process. The list of key aspects of the process below will help guide you to a successful orientation for your new employee:

> The manager is responsible for successful orientation of a new employee into organization
> You must allocate time to do a thorough job
> Engage in advance planning; get out the calendar; get organized
> Use a standard orientation checklist
> Follow the plan you have developed and/or the organization's prescribed process
> Consistency between departments and managers is important so share your plans with others
> Your involvement as the hiring manager is critical
> Designate the best match for Advisor and Trainer(s)
> Create a welcoming environment for the new employee
> Provide the tools necessary to build employee success

Although there may be administrative support for the orientation process to get the checklist started; take an active role in making sure the orientation is providing the introductions you feel are needed to do a complete job for the new employee. There should be little difference in on-boarding for permanent employees versus long-term temporary or contract workers as they will all need to receive an orientation to the organization and your department to be successful. The new employee will be better connected in the process and will demonstrate more responsibility and assertiveness if you make them responsible for owning the orientation checklist. This enables them to develop a relationship with the people they are meeting with which is essential to their future success. Allow the new employee to adjust their orientation schedule as needed while checking off tasks as they are completed. Have the new employee turn in the completed orientation checklist to you when finished. This gives you the opportunity to review the new employee's orientation experience with them to ensure that everything has been covered. Make sure that you follow-up and address any outstanding issues or questions.

Include in the orientation a discussion between you and the new employee regarding expectations and requirements for the work setting. Include proper care and conduct in dealing with others and the proper approach to use in dealing with specific work situations. Rules and regulations are very important; establish the importance of following work guidelines and provide an open environment for the employee to ask questions, share concerns and report things that seem out of place.

Last but not least; identify objectives for the new employee and establish a psychological contract. A psychological contract is the set of expectations held by the individual and specifying what the individual and the organization expect to give to and receive from one another in the course of their working relationship. This mental contract is very powerful and can last a lifetime in the mind of the new employee. All people require an answer as to why they were chosen to a position and if not provided by the manager, the brain will fill in the blanks with whatever the person feels is the best answer. This is a huge opportunity for you to get a new person grounded on the reasons you hired them and how their skills are best suited to handle the specific goals and needs that you must accomplish. The beginning is where this needs to occur to be optimal; adjusting or correcting the contract at a later point in time may be difficult to accomplish. I will never forget the many conversations with workers who after thirty or forty years of employment with the company would cite a reference to the boss that originally hired them because they were a hard worker. The psychological contract is a binding agreement that provides people a strong sense of belonging and purpose over their entire career linked to a single instance or comment during the transaction of the hiring process. Never underestimate the power of this within the hearts and minds of the people you work with.

New Employee Training

Once all orientation tasks are complete, you will want to review the progress of the new hire and determine if any further orientation is required. Depending on the job and the new employee's experience you will also need to develop a detailed training plan and calendar so that the new hire goes straight from orientation into job training and productive work. Choosing the right trainer(s) and allocating their time to the process is a critical next step and one that should be prepared in advance of the new employee hire date.

Effective training is fundamental to new employee success. There are four key areas in the process of basic training: 1) Explain, 2) Demonstrate, 3) Observe, and 4) Review. Even though all people learn different things at varied paces the training process basically follows the same four steps in the sequence noted to be deemed successful or complete.

Basic learning occurs in everyone through a series of training experiences. The new employee will learn the most through a direct or tangible experience. It is painful to go through the first week on the job spending your time listening to others talk about what they do. The best way to learn something is to do something. Once the new employee has experienced the activity they can reflect on the experience and make comparisons to what they have learned in previous work experiences. Through a combination of new experiences and reflections the new employee will develop impressions and patterns of thought regarding how things are done in the new work environment. This series of experiences provide an abstract view of the workplace through the conceptualization of the yet to be experienced aspects of the new environment. With a clear idea of what to do based upon what the new employee has experienced, observed, and conceptualized the new employee will take action and experiment with the work they do.

Complete learning happens when the learner moves through all four stages (tangible experience, reflection, conceptualization, and action/experimentation) and the new knowledge, skills, and/or attitudes become the basis for new behavior.

30/60/90 reviews are a very effective way of developing a positive working relationship with your new employee. As a manager you need to schedule a brief checkpoint meeting on the calendar with the new employee for 30, 60, & 90 days.

- ✓ 30 days: review the completed orientation form with new employee and discuss any questions the new employee has
- ✓ 60 days: review the comfort level with new employee adjusting to new work environment; follow-up on training process to see if the new employee is grasping the position
- ✓ 90 days: review the success of the training process and assess the new employee's ability to settle into the position; assess the new employee's satisfaction with the position and organization

Getting to know your employee on a personal level is important especially to a new person. A newly hired employee needs to know that they are welcome and appreciated for their decision to work in your company. Everyone wants to belong to something and feel good about what they contribute to the organization. As humans we gauge our level of importance and the value that the organization places on us based upon the relationship developed between ourselves and our manager. A manager who takes time to share stories and experiences with their employees demonstrates that they care about what their people do and the value they bring to the organization.

A professional manager cares and shows that they care by investing their time in guiding, listening, confiding in and supporting the people that they hire. This is important for all employees whether recently hired or not; however, it is very important that this relationship and level of understanding and appreciation is established with newly hired employees to bind their support and performance in team and individual achievement.

A professional manager's action is his/her mission; the mission is appropriate action.

Chapter 4 – Use Rules, Regulations, and Policies

As a manager it is your responsibility to know the company's rules and regulations, policies and code of conduct. It is important that you set the example for adherence to the rules and guidelines established by the company for the management of the work environment. It is also critical that you use rules, regulations, and policies properly and maintain a balance between rule administration and employee relations.

As a young supervisor I was once given the task of reading the work rules to my Union employees during a weekly meeting. It was an awkward experience and I will never forget how belittling it seemed for me and for the employees to go through this process. In fact, I had to make sure that everyone received a copy and I had to check off that everyone got their rules. I observed many of them throwing the document in the break-room trashcan as they left the meeting!

Years later as a manger I went through numerous grievance procedures and arbitrations and remember how important it was that the company could prove through documentation that every employee had received the work rules and had them read to them. Had we missed any employees or groups within the facility the discipline issued to the grievant could have been dismissed and reversed due to inconsistent and unfair treatment. Even though the person disciplined had clearly violated the rules, the arbitrator would decide in favor of the employee if management was unable to prove all aspects of managerial correctness. It is a sinking feeling when you are ripped to shreds by a Union Business Agent and then must sit through the disappointment of a hearing panel dismissing and reversing your discipline because of a technicality that you could not defend. I had this experience too many times in my early career as a manager and learned how to avoid the embarrassment. I learned the cold hard fact that it always needs to be proven (via documentation) that management behavior has been applied consistently and comprehensively to seal the armor; any slight crack in the armor and the case will be broken. It still did not seem fair at the time but it sold me on the importance of maintaining and communicating work rules in the organization.

Rules and Regulations

All employees are expected to observe certain guidelines covering behavior, attitude, quality of work, and overall performance while on the premises of the company or on any occasion when representing the company. Rules and regulations are not designed to restrict employee actions, but to encourage teamwork, maintain the standards of all employees, cement good relationships between team members, managers, and between employees and customers. All employees must receive and review the rules and regulations during their orientation; they are to be studied and used as a part of their daily work routine.

Rules and regulations are generally divided into two categories: Group 1 are considered the most serious violations and employees violating them are subject to immediate discharge; the second group, Group 2, are less serious and managers are encouraged to follow normal disciplinary procedures when dealing with employee violations. Here are some basic rules that all managers should be familiar with and understand:

Group 1

The following are generally considered Group 1 work rule violations (for the specific list of company work rules consult your company or organization's employee handbook):

1. Possession of: firearms, weapons, or any kind of drugs or intoxicants on company premises or in vehicles.
2. Falsification of any reports or records including employment, personnel, absence, sickness, sales, or inventory records, etc.
3. False claims of injury.
4. Misuse or removal from the premises without proper written authorization of company property, records, merchandise, or any other materials.
5. Fighting on company premises, or while on duty in any location.
6. Dishonesty.
7. Immoral conduct or indecency on company property.
8. Punching any timecard, or work record, of any other employee.
9. Insubordinate conduct or refusal to follow manager's instructions, including threatening, intimidating, coercing, or using abusive language to fellow employees, supervisors, customers, or visitors.
10. Restricting operations or interference with others in the performance of their jobs or engaging or participating in any interruption of work or operations.
11. Reporting to work in an unfit physical condition.

12. Neglect of job duties and responsibilities, or failure or refusal to perform assigned work.
13. Carrying unauthorized passengers in company vehicles or using company vehicles for personal use, or being a passenger in a company vehicle unless authorized by the manager.

Group 2

1. Failure to be at the appointed work place, ready to work, properly dressed, at the regular starting time and failure to remain at such work place and at work until the regular quitting time.
2. Failure to remain on his/her job assignment until the end of his/her scheduled hours, or until relieved by the supervisor on duty.
3. Use of telephones for personal calls or conducting personal business during working hours.
4. Smoking in non-designated areas.
5. Carelessly handling, throwing, or damaging merchandise or littering work areas.
6. Violation of any safety rules or common safety practices or engaging in any conduct which tends to create a safety hazard.
7. Horseplay.
8. Abuse or destruction of company property, tools, equipment, or merchandise.
9. Unauthorized or unexcused absences or lateness.
10. Illicit gambling activities.
11. Unlawful or improper conduct, outside of the company premises or during non-working hours, which affects the employee's relationship to his/her job, fellow employees, supervision, or the company's

products, property, reputation, or good will in the community.

12. Failure to wear or use required safety equipment and immediately report to manager any injury or accident.
13. Failure to be responsible for all company's equipment and property assigned to or requisitioned by the employee in his/her custody and care.
14. Use of other than the company entrance designated for his/her use.
15. Entering or remaining on company premises unless on duty, scheduled for work, or authorized by manager.
16. Failure to permit inspection of any package, lunch container, purse, handbag, or vehicle at the time of entering or leaving the company's premises.
17. Leaving one's assigned area of work without specific permission from manager.
18. Failure to report an expected absence or give the reasons for inability to work to supervisor or designated representative at least one hour in advance of his/her scheduled beginning hours of work.
19. Failure to use only the parking facility designated for his/her use.
20. Failure to notify in writing immediately of any change in personal data.
21. Causing waste or litter and contributing to poor housekeeping, unsanitary or unsafe conditions. (Eating or drinking in any non-designated area is strictly prohibited in some production and storage areas for companies in food related industries.)
22. Unsatisfactory work performance.

23. Solicitation for any cause during working hours on company premises without prior written approval from manager.
24. Repeated garnishment of his/her wages.
25. Punching in more than five (5) minutes before normal starting time or five (5) minutes after normal quitting time, unless approved by a member of supervision who shall initial the entry.
26. Discourtesy to customers or suppliers.

The foregoing rules are not intended to be all-inclusive. The seriousness or nature of the offense may place a Group 2 offense in Group 1. All rules and regulations documents should include language that states the company shall, when it considers appropriate, establish additional rules deemed necessary as a result of operational requirements. An employee who fails to maintain at all times proper standards of conduct or who violates any of the preceding rules may subject himself/herself to disciplinary action, up to and including discharge.

The guidelines encompassed in the rules and regulations document serve to provide a safe, honest, and ethical work environment for both employees and customers. These professional standards must be observed. The observation of these guidelines will enable everyone to function on their jobs properly and efficiently.

Policies

You need to be familiar with and know how to access the company's policies and procedures. Generally, these are covered with new employees in their orientation provided by the Human Resource department and referenced in the employee handbook. As a manager you are responsible for maintaining the integrity of the workplace and your knowledge of and support of the company policies is very important. Some of the policies that you should be aware of fall into the following subject areas: Safety and Health, Security, Emergency Response, Weather and other time-off or operation closure guidelines, Equal Employment Opportunity, Affirmative Action, Drug Policy, Sexual Harassment, Workplace Harassment, Workplace Violence, Absenteeism and Tardiness, Holiday and Vacation, Leave of Absence (multiple policies; e.g. Military, FMLA, Medical, Bereavement, Jury Duty, Voting, etc.), Work Related Injury and Workers Compensation, Company Property, Acceptable Use of Information Assets, Electronic Communication and Devises, Confidentiality, Travel and Expense, Payroll and Timekeeping.

Other areas to be aware of and understand are: Wellness and Assistance programs, Severance Policy, Disability, Benefits, Performance Review and Compensation Guidelines, Incentive/Bonus Plan, Internal Job Posting process/procedure, and Education Reimbursement.

The most important policy to read and understand is the company Code of Conduct. You must be familiar with the code and know where to find the document when a situation arises that you need to review and account for. The ability of a company to maintain ethical business practices is based on everyone's compliance to the code. This is a critical component of success and all aspects of the business falling under the jurisdiction of the code and your compliance to the code is extremely serious and important.

I visited a partner company once that had invited our team to tour their facility and office complex. The company was a new business that had been growing rapidly and doing a great job servicing the market in their segment. The owner of the business was the president and founder and at the point we met with them he had fifty percent of the shares of the company. The president guided us on the tour and when he showed us the human resource department he commented on how many people they were hiring and training each week to keep up with the volume. He then made a gender reference that I won't repeat that did not sit well with me. A little further along the tour he showed us a breakroom that had alcohol on tap for the employees (the business was not a brewery)! In the restroom there were sexually explicit pictures (not valued works of art like you would see in a museum) on the walls which again did not seem appropriate.

I don't know of any lawsuits resulting from the company that we visited; however I wonder what example that set for the managers and employees in the firm. It is possible that violating a basic code of civility may not result in immediate or even long-term problems for a person or organization, but it only takes once! It only takes one lawsuit to destroy the manager's reputation and tarnish the company name forever. Whether there is a risk of a problem occurring from this behavior should not be the issue. The main issue is why engage in bad conduct in the first place! A professional manager sets a good example through his/her behavior; not just once, not in certain circumstances, but all of the time.

Last but not least is the importance of knowing the company's Mission Statement and Value Statement. Having key values that represent the company is important; knowing what these key values are and sharing them with your employees is also important; but living the values in your daily life is what we are ultimately responsible for as managers of the company. I spoke with a close friend and previous colleague about how the environment at our previous company had changed after bringing in another new management team. Over a period of ten years and multiple changes senior management lost sight of the Value Statement. He told me that the company had installed surveillance cameras in all the facilities and started disciplining people if they stopped work for a minute to talk to a fellow worker. They now discipline people if they arrive at break one minute early or leave one minute late. Just like robots the employees are expected to jump immediately when the break buzzer rings.

The environment has turned from being a highly productive and proud workforce to a group of experienced and senior people who are angry and frustrated with the company. According to my friend it is hard to go to work every day and come home to the family feeling good and happy about what they do and who they work for. Instead of producing at 100% or more of the engineered standard the vast majority of the long-term employees are dropping down to the bare minimum of 95% and some are dropping even lower and increasing only when they have to.

Why? Because the new management team has created a prison environment! It is this type of behavior that insults and tarnishes the manager title. This new team of people attempting to run the company is not really managers; rather they are running the company into the ground due their lack of management and their ignorance of the Value Statement.

It is the behavior of the managers and leaders in the company that determines the culture of the company and shapes who and what the company is all about. The mission of the organization is the accomplishment of the basic culture that is established by the attention and focus placed on key aspects of the business. How those components are truly valued and proven to be important in the eyes of employees and customers is determined by the actions taken every day by the leaders of the organization.

A professional manager's action is his/her mission; the mission is appropriate action.

Rules are like protective walls; those that stay inside them are safe; those who tear them down risk harm to the community inside them.

Chapter 5 – Team Discipline

Applying Discipline

Discipline is a means of maintaining good order and conduct in any group of people. When facing an employee disciplinary situation, a professional manager must engage in well defined communication and follow specific guidelines to deal effectively with the subject of employee discipline. A professional manager must make sure that they understand what the intent and purpose of the discipline is before taking action. Remember the story about the manager's armor, if there is a crack in the logic for the discipline applied, the discipline will be rendered ineffective. Manager action and intent must fall within one of the following categories; and must progress in the order listed below whereas the only legitimate reasons for employee discipline are emphasized:

1. To improve and correct behavior (this is the number one reason to apply discipline and should account for 90 percent of discipline issued)
2. To set an example of one to deter many (is an important element to maintaining discipline in a group of people however must only be used as needed and in the correct manner)
3. To get rid of undesirable employees (should only be used as a last resort)

Let's make sure we understand the true meaning of discipline. The definition of discipline can be related to the guidelines and details required to study in an area of emphasis in the process of becoming proficient in that area. A discipline is an area of study; biology, commerce, crafts, medicine, karate, mathematics, sociology, etc. where we accept certain truths and work within guiding principles as members of the group. Staying true to our principles is acting within our discipline in accordance with our study and beliefs.

Discipline as applied in a workplace setting is all about maintaining the guidelines required for the business to achieve its intended purpose. To go outside of the discipline of the organization is to violate the truth that the team subscribes to when engaging in the practice and furthering the growth and enrichment of the cause. A system of discipline within the organization maintains the behavior of the individuals that comprise the organization within the accepted boundaries of what determines whether the entity will exist as designed, perish to another form, or dissipate entirely.

Employees should know the expected standards (rules) of conduct. There are two general categories:

1. Acts prohibited by society in general both inside and outside the workplace
2. Acts which are acceptable in outside society but prohibited at work

A dictatorship may not be an acceptable form of government outside of the workforce, but within the four walls of the company, it may be management's way or the highway! That does not imply that a dictatorial style of management is the best; I believe that it is not. Stopping and then turning right on red on our city streets may be acceptable and legal, but on the property of a company whereby rules determine a construction vehicle or material handling piece of equipment must remain stopped until the light turns green is a correct and appropriate standard. You may have the right to ride a motorcycle without a helmet, or work on your personal property without a hardhat, but on the company jobsite operating certain machinery may require a helmet and being present in the work area may require wearing a hardhat. Perfectly acceptable and legal behavior outside of the workplace could result in termination inside the workplace. Knowing the difference and recognizing that there is a difference should be perfectly acceptable in our society.

When applying rules and regulations in the workplace you need to be cognizant of a few key items to help you with effective use of company guidelines:

Protect rules. Don't negotiate away your management rights to issue, modify, and enforce rules. Don't condone violations of rules or establish precedents that conflict and delineate written rules.

Publicize and communicate rules. For written rules use the bulletin board, intra-net site or shared directories, and employee handbook or orientation booklet. For verbal rules (kept to a minimum) use employee meetings and make the notes available to the team; in either case re-issue every year to keep fresh and maintain level of importance.

Don't list penalties. The unexpected is the most effective . . . employees need not know exactly what will happen to them, merely that discipline will be given. Past experience will dictate the "appropriateness" of the penalty.

You as manager must have the authority to enforce rules. The manager must maintain control and respect of the workforce. The manager must be trained in disciplinary concepts. The opportunity must exist for upward management consultation.

Remember, that it is your responsibility to enforce the rules. Not only is it important that the rules are enforced but that the manner in which you as a manager deal with a person who has violated the rules is viewed as fair and appropriate. Your approach is important not only in the context of what the business requires and what the company policies prescribe, but also in the eyes of the employees; especially the employees referred to as the "silent majority". When you enforce rules in the right way, the "silent majority" will support you as a manager even though you may never hear them tell you that. Don't let the "noisy minority" influence your actions as a manager to the detriment of the "silent majority" who quietly go about doing a great job for you every day, day in and day out, supporting you in your efforts to lead them. If the "silent majority" agree with "how" you have treated people and determine in their minds that you have been fair, then you will maintain rule integrity and also maintain your managerial credibility.

Just Cause

All discipline must be reviewed under the "Just Cause" concept. In order to proceed with discipline, you must ask yourself several key questions and review your answers under the following pretense so that you are prepared to make the right disciplinary decisions:

Did the employee commit the offense? Facts, not opinions, are important because the parties are equals in an arbitration procedure. Remember the company always has the burden of proof.

Did the offense warrant discipline? This is not considering degree of discipline but whether any at all is justified. What are the mitigating circumstances? Was the rule communicated? Has the standard been enforced or ignored? Did the manager provoke the employee's act?

Does the punishment fit the crime? You must consider the past record of the employee. Has it been documented? Was the offense similar to a previous offense? Consistency is the key, not uniformity; the latter implies that an employee's past record is meaningless . . . it is not.

It is always helpful in all disciplinary situations to think about your decisions and actions as if you were preparing for a future arbitration or hearing and would be required to explain your decision to a judge or arbitrator. This is a great way of making sure you have provided the correct and complete compilation of documentation and can easily guide another through the detail to the justification for the discipline decision. The following checklist has been used in the past to prepare for arbitration hearings to determine if "Just Cause" exists for disciplinary action. A "No" answer to any of the seven test questions normally indicates that "Just Cause" does not exist.

Just Cause Checklist

✓ Has the employer given the employee advance warning of the possible or probable disciplinary consequences of the conduct?

✓ Is the employer's rule or managerial order reasonably related to the efficient and safe operation of the business?

✓ Before administering discipline, has the employer made the effort to discover whether the employee did, in fact, violate a rule or order of management?

✓ Has the employer's investigation been conducted fairly and objectively?

✓ Has the investigation produced substantial evidence or proof that the employee is guilty as charged?

✓ Has the company applied its rules, orders, and penalties evenhandedly and without discrimination?

✓ Is the degree of discipline considered in this particular case reasonably related to?
   1. The seriousness of the employee's proven offense?
   2. The record of the employee in his/her service with the company?

If you find that there are chinks in the armor because some of the answers are "No"; now is the time to correct before proceeding. Moving further along the path of discipline with holes in the armor will cause the situation to get worse and possibly backfire in the end. What you lose by taking a step backward in the process to rectify a situation is minimal by comparison to what you could lose if you proceed and ignore a failure of the "Just Cause" evaluation. Not only could you lose the case, but you may make it harder to apply discipline in the future and you may run the risk of losing credibility with the workforce. A professional manager uses a problem caught in the checklist process to bring forward a weakness, not back away from the issue, assume responsibility and correct the problem. Again, problems will beget profits in this process as well when handled properly.

Progressive Discipline

Progressive discipline means that an employee's entire record of previous rule violations and disciplinary action is taken into account when new discipline is being considered. This also determines what level of discipline to apply as the consequence of a new violation of conduct occurs. Let's say that you have a warehouse employee who has a quality issue when it comes to order selection and tends to pick the wrong item for the customer. Every time this employee's weekly mispick percentage is above the acceptable threshold he/she could receive discipline for that. Discipline issued for the first occurrence would be a casual discussion. Over time the discipline could progress to other levels up to and eventually leading to discharge if the employee does not make the necessary improvements.

Generally progressive discipline follows a path that includes multiple steps in an effort to work to improve and correct employee behavior. Mostly Group 2 rule violations progress in this manner similar to the example of the warehouse selector that has a mispick problem. An important distinction is that a Group 1 violation depending upon the severity of the issue may result in immediate discharge regardless of the employee's record.

Back to our warehouse employee for a second; if the order selector not only has a mispick problem but also has a performance problem in that they are not achieving the selection standard or quota for a specific week, they could receive discipline for that Group 2 work rule violation also. When there are two or more Group 2 violations occurring at the same time, all the violation types are combined to determine the next level of discipline. Each separate rule violation does not track on its own separate progressive discipline course. The warehouse employee would not be at level three for mispicks while at the same time level one for performance.

Let's break this down further: if in the first week the employee missed the quality threshold they would receive level one discipline for that week. If in the second week they missed the production quota they would receive the level two discipline step for that week. If in the third week they missed both the quality and production requirements they would receive a discipline document describing both violations and receive a single discipline at level three. Some work settings and corresponding work requirements will follow a weekly schedule, others may be monthly, or even tied to project time periods; many will only count a rolling 12 months. In any case the progressive discipline model works in the same way.

Although progressive discipline for Group 2 rule violations may include any and all violations regardless of the rule violated, when attendance issues surface as the basis of the recent violation, the progressive discipline model may focus solely on the attendance issues separately. There is a tendency with attendance issues that there may be other external factors impacting the work behavior that may need special support and attention. Separating the progressive discipline corrective action for attendance may be required for the employee to get back on their feet and capable of being effective at their job.

The following list is an example of progressive discipline; again, the severity of the violations may alter this process to fewer steps depending upon the circumstances:

1. Training (Has it occurred and is it documented?)
2. *Casual Discussion* (Documented by manager)
3. *Casual Discussion* (Documented by manager)
4. *Written Reprimand* *
5. *Casual Discussion* (Documented by manager)
6. *Written Reprimand* * *(also referred to as Final Written Warning)*
7. *Suspension?*
8. Termination

* When a written reprimand is given the following statement must be made clear and should be included in the document: "Future violations of company rules and regulations may result in further discipline up to and including discharge."

All levels of discipline, especially initial casual discussions, should include a comment about the consequences of future rules violations in that further discipline may occur. It is important to note that the time period between two levels of discipline must allow enough time for the employee to be able to improve their performance. As a manager you cannot issue discipline back-to-back without ample work time between the time periods measured and the physical ability of the employee to work on making an improvement. For instance, if the employee violates a rule in week one but goes on vacation or is off work in week two, they might not receive the discipline until week three. If they in turn violate a rule in week three prior to receiving the discipline for week one, they cannot then receive discipline in week four for the violation that occurred in week three. Of course, it depends on the work violation, if it is a Group 1 violation immediate action must be taken. If it is a Group 2 violation for missing a weekly production or quality threshold you must allow enough time on the job between discipline levels to demonstrate that you are giving the employee the time needed to improve their work performance.

In some situations an additional step is added prior to termination whereby the employee is suspended from one day up to a week to be given additional time to think through the implications of their actions in a final attempt to let the employee know the seriousness of their behavior and provide clear direction and opportunity for improvement before actual termination occurs. This also helps solidify your case if it does result in a termination that is protested and taken into a hearing, arbitration, or litigation.

An interesting thought to keep in mind: you never really win an employee lawsuit. Even if the judgment is in your favor, legal costs are very expensive. Other costs include employee morale problems, employee turnover, psychological or emotional drain on the organization, loss of productivity in other areas and loss of business focus or momentum. Of course, there are exceptions to this but generally going down a legal path does not provide a winning solution.

Have you heard the expression that leaving a wound to fester does not make it better? When you have an employee performance problem you must address it immediately or it could get worse. The longer you wait to confront the situation the more difficult it will be for the employee to accept the position you take as a manger to correct the condition. If allowed to continue for a long period of time an employee may feel that they are in the right because "they have always done it this way." The employee's reaction might be one of shock in that they cannot see why their behavior is a problem all of a sudden especially if the behavior has been ignored or condoned in the past.

To effectively address and resolve issues with employee behavior you must act quickly. Start by confronting the employee to address the specific behavior. Give the employee a chance to explain the behavior from their perspective. Be clear in your explanation of the company policy and/or the expectation you have as manager for the employee for future behavior. As you are discussing the situation make sure you take notes of the conversation in the presence of the employee so that they are made aware of the seriousness of the situation and the efforts you are making to accurately represent and document the issue.

As you work to shape and correct employee behavior through the progressive discipline process it is important that you use conflict resolution and effective confrontation skills. The key is to get the employee out of denial and into a place that they can recognize the need for a change in their behavior.

Capturing and documenting the conversation with the employee regarding the facts surrounding the situation is an important step in the resolution process.

Facts, Objectives, Solutions, and Actions

As mentioned above facts are critical to documenting an employee performance issue and bringing an employee to the realization of the need for a change in behavior. Goals and plans for improvement need to be objective and related to the expectations that the company has for people in their work responsibilities. The manager should offer the right mix of sources for employee consideration that address the situation and strive to be effective in providing solutions and suggestions to help an employee succeed. Communication from the manager needs to represent action related to what steps are going to be considered toward improvement in a situation and what the consequences are if the behavior does not improve.

Facts

As a professional manager you produce effective documentation and understand the importance of objectivity. Facts are critical to provide an objective description of employee behavior and to help frame up the situation. Facts are needed to properly represent the specific employee behavior. Facts help provide documentation that create a platform devoid of emotion or doubt about what the root cause of the issue really is.

Facts include: Who, What, When, Where, and Why. Facts are based in what we can: Hear, See, Touch, Taste, and Smell. If your documentation consists of opinions and speculation it might as well be thrown in the trash. In the process of documenting the facts do not worry about grammar, spelling, the way the sentences flow, etc. You are not writing a book or an essay. Noting the specific details in the sequence mentioned above even if handwritten on a scrap piece of paper is more valuable than a nicely typed document that has been written after the fact. The latter leads to concerns that a document produced too far removed from the incident may have been contrived or manipulated to the manager's benefit. This may not be true however; we are dealing with employee and even possibly a judge's perception of the truth behind the incident or argument, so it is important that you get the facts right.

When gathering the facts around a situation always make sure that you are looking for and capturing both positive and negative examples of employee behavior. Always keep the facts specific to an effect or result of the employee behavior, for instance: "The result of the error in the report you created cost the company $xx." Use third-party statements as facts to consider in the process, for example: "Two other people saw you on the third floor talking about xxxxx on xx/xx/xxxx at approximately x:xx pm." An important source of facts for your consideration is the employee comments and responses to questions you ask them concerning the issue. Effective listening will make you a better investigator in these situations.

I had a boss approach me once and in the discussion he cited a statement made by another manager who did not interact with me or work with me at all. The comment that the other manager made was basically an opinion and referred to the broader department's lack of ability to predict something. The item that had not been communicated to us had become an obvious and well-known failure of the other team to communicate in a situation that coincidentally emanated from the other manager's department. Somehow the opinion was twisted into an example of how I failed to execute on the unknown! Here was a boss providing an assessment of my performance that was removed from the environment in the first place and in addition did not have any facts to make an assessment of what really happened. Unfortunately, this is not an uncommon experience for many people. As a professional manager you do not go on a last-minute scramble to create facts or use other people's opinions to complete a performance assessment. The last thing you ever want to be perceived as by your employees is the manager who puts too much reliance on and makes decisions based on other people's opinions. A professional manager knows the people that report to him/her. They use facts to guide conclusions and engage in discussions throughout the year to beget profits. They know when someone is stating a fact or hiding behind an opinion. Facts are very powerful when used correctly.

I had the opportunity to receive credit for an accomplishment in a meeting with senior managers when I least expected it from a boss that I worked for who was a professional manager. It was during a project where I had pioneered a new process for a distribution initiative and although not completely satisfied and not completely done with the project, I felt that we were making great improvements. When my boss spoke about the process I was implementing he cited a few facts surrounding the project and numbers associated with the initial improvement that slammed home to the group listening that not only were we going to get to a better place operationally, but that I deserved the credit for the achievement. The way that the manager used facts made a significant positive impression on me and the people in the room. It was easy for people to connect the facts and believe that this was more than just one person's opinion of the merits of the project. Never underestimate the importance of using facts properly and getting your facts straight to build your management credibility.

Objectives

Objectives are necessary to shape and correct employee behavior. Properly constructed objectives provide a roadmap for an employee to follow to improvement. A basic "How To" for correcting a problem resulting from an engagement between an employee and manager that results in a well documented and designed objective or set of objectives will help an employee correct a specific problem with their behavior.

As a professional manager you want to include the employee in developing the objective(s). Allow the employee to suggest possible goals and objectives for themselves. As a manager you must set the objective one way or another, but it is always best if you ask the employee to offer an objective and ask for their support in working together to establish one.

It is critical that you include the following elements in your improvement plan and that the objectives developed are: specific, designed to support a positive approach to the problem, established as a requirement and not an option, and thorough and complete with no holes or loopholes.

Solutions

As a manager you want to use solutions as a resource and also a means of demonstrating that you are actively coaching an employee toward achievement. Unlike objectives which are requirements, an employee is not required to use a solution but should be encouraged to do so by the manager to be successful. Remember solutions are a necessary method for an employee to accomplish their goals and objectives.

A manager and/or employee can utilize a variety of resources including training courses, books, specific alternative work experiences, on-line courses, individuals that can be used as a resource, and other creative ideas that the manager and employee can devise to help.

The wrong way to approach an employee is to tell them that they need to fix the problem. The correct way is to make suggestions about programs and resources that can be or are available to them to consider working toward improvement. As a professional manager a good approach is to provide a personal reference to how you might handle the situation to provide support and direction to the employee.

Actions

Actions are a must if a manager is to drive an improvement in employee behavior. An action sets the expectation, direction and communication to the employee from the manager as to the action that will be taken by the manager if the problem behavior continues. Actions set the tone and provide the message of how serious the problem is and the importance of getting it corrected.

Specific action steps and dialogue directed in the correct manner is required to shape the behavior and must include several key elements. The current disciplinary action must clearly describe the type and nature of the discipline and what level it represents. Discussion concerning potential future disciplinary action must be clear in that the employee may be subjected to further discipline up to and including discharge. As a manager follow-up is critical to make sure that the behavior is changing in the correct direction. Specific guidelines and detailed documentation are required to identify task completion goal dates, follow-up discussion, and review dates. It is also important to follow-up to obtain proof that the employee is acknowledging and applying the new training or methods acquired in the process. Ultimately you need to follow-up to ensure that the employee is incorporating the required change in their actions and behavior.

As a manager you must take action. You may do everything right up to this point and fail in the end because appropriate action is not taken. Appropriate action is timely. It is handled in a decisive and determined manner with serious intent. Remember substance without action is nothing; action without substance is disaster.

Analyzing Your Approach

In this section we have talked about facts, objectives, solutions, and actions. We have also discussed the manager's responsibility to make sure that management is doing its job properly in a given situation. We have also discussed the importance of documentation and working with the employee to clearly identify the problem behavior that needs to improve for the employee to be successful. Before proceeding in the process a professional manager must analyze the situation and make sure that everything has been accounted for. Discipline should not be considered until the analysis has been completed. The key question you need to ask yourself as a manager is whether your actions are sufficient to support the improvement process. What are the key components in your plan to develop discipline to support the improvement plan?

Items that you need to consider for analyzing your approach to the employee disciplinary process includes an assessment of thoughts surrounding what you feel the perspective of the employee is in the situation. Does the employee know they are being helped and do they know they have a problem? Do you feel that the employee knows how to remedy the issue? Does the employee realize their job may be at risk? Does the employee recognize that it is the manager's objective to create an opportunity for them to succeed?

If the answers to these questions are "No" then you as manager need to go back to work following the principles in this section to get alignment with the employee concerning the situation and behavior that needs to improve. Remember what we said at the beginning about the manager's armor, if there is a crack in the logic for the discipline applied, the discipline will be rendered ineffective.

Sample Written Reprimand (Warning Letter)

To: xxxx
From: xxxxx, Manager
Re: Written Warning

On xx/xx/xxxx and on xx/xx/xxxx I counseled you about your xxxx performance and cautioned you that further performance issues may lead to formal disciplinary action. On xx/xx/xxxx I gave you a Verbal Warning regarding your xxxx performance at work. The Verbal Warning was based on the fact that you failed to achieve the work required of you in that you did (or did not) do xxxx on xx/xx/xxxx and also failed to perform assigned work on xx/xx/xxxx, xx/xx/xxxx, and xx/xx/xxxx. I told you that you needed to perform at xxxx level and complete xxxx work satisfactorily. I also cautioned you that any additional performance problems with xxxx may lead to further disciplinary action.

On xx/xx/xxxx you failed to perform xxxx at an acceptable level. Company Rule #x states: "xxxxxxxxxxxxx." I expect you to perform xxxx at an acceptable level. We have discussed several solutions that you might consider to assist you in your performance improvement; I suggest that you take advantage of these solutions to correct any performance issues that you have.

This written warning will be placed in your personnel file. If you do not meet the performance objectives I have outlined in this letter, you may be subjected to further disciplinary action, up to and including termination.

I have received a copy of this letter:
Employee Name: _____ Date: _____

Documentation is a story; make sure it is historical and not a work of fiction.

Chapter 6 – Organization and Documentation

Documenting Performance Issues

One of the most important questions you need to ask yourself before working with an employee to improve performance is: has management done its job managing? All situations can be different so you must review and analyze the situation first and determine the underlying problem. In order to answer the question about whether management has done its job or not the situation and the record of the offense and previous offenses must be clearly documented.

Why is documentation so important? Without documentation you might as well assume that it didn't happen. I know this sounds harsh, but the burden of proof is always on management to prove that the behavior occurred, and that management took the correct steps in working with the employee to improve the situation. The value of time spent documenting the situation properly will reveal itself numerous times in future situations as a benefit to you as a manager. Today's work environment is getting more complicated and documentation is a crucial part of dealing with employee issues. There are some basic and important aspects of documentation to consider that will assist you as a professional manager:

Most important to the business, documentation must be used effectively by the manager to create an opportunity for the employee to succeed. This is the number one goal of documentation and when the wording portrays that intent it is much more effective.

To be legally defendable documentation must be objective. Opinions cannot bleed through the wording surrounding the information captured or the case will be lost. Documentation must also demonstrate consistency for legal purposes. Remember that from a legal perspective documentation represents proof of what really happened. The closer the documentation represents the actual situation the more acceptable the testimony and defendable the case will be.

Manager's Employee File

Organization is one of the keys to be a successful manager. For every employee reporting directly to you it is a good practice to maintain a manager's employee file. This is different than the file that Human Resources maintain for every employee. The manager's employee file may consist of a physical folder kept locked in your desk or file cabinet or it may be an electronic folder kept on a secure drive to protect confidentiality.

The manager's employee file should consist of the following items: Employee performance goals and the most recent evaluations. Any notes from performance review discussions. Any performance improvement plans (PIP's). Individual employee development plans.

Weekly or monthly performance data is also a key part of the employee file. This may include information that has been discussed with the employee, or it may be progress notes and updates provided by the employee.

Of course documentation is stored in the file. All documents need to be dated and author identified; all written documents should be signed by author. This includes notes on issues discussed with the employee and back-up and supporting documentation. All written narrative on performance discussions (also known as Casual discussions) and all Discipline letters and employee reprimands are included in the file. Absence reports may be stored separately or may also be placed in the employee file.

The file should also be used for all supporting documentation. A primary source of reference material to include in the file is: completed orientation checklist, training documents and checklists, job description, and observation notes. Comments and notes from others regarding employee behavior (good and bad) should be included. As a reference for specific communication and directives that are relevant to employee accountability all meeting minutes and notes should be included in the file or stored separately with the date of the meeting and names of all participants listed on the document. Documentation regarding discussions or training on policies, procedures, and rules should also be in the employee file.

As humans we want to have people recognize us for the good things we have done. An ideal employee file from an employee's perspective is one that is empty. Our thoughts surrounding an employee file in the hands of our manager elicit past failures, weaknesses, documents that speak to the things we have done that we are not proud of or we believe were placed in the file unfairly without our ability to rebuke the information or state our viewpoint in whatever the negative situation was.

As a professional manager the employee file is proof that the employees have been trained well, have performed well at their tasks, have been counseled when needed, have engaged in development activities to support their performance and career growth, and that the manager is fair and consistent in his/her evaluation of the workforce. A manager's employee file should never be an unresolved or contested collection of documents that the employee is either unaware of or feels does not represent the facts of a given situation. A file is nothing to hide from the employee, rather it should be accepted that the file exists and that it is in the employees benefit that fair and equitable facts are stored by the manager on the record of all employee's performance.

A professional manager, who conducts himself/herself in a manner that is open and honest, supportive and caring, fair and consistent, maintains a psychological employee file in the minds of the employees. All employees resolve that the manager regards them with a high level of trust and concern for their wellbeing and in turn the employees regard their manager with a high level of trust as well. If the employees believe that their manager's decisions will always be based on facts and not opinions, on truth and not hearsay, on logic and not feelings, on their ability to do the work versus a popularity contest, when all employees are engaged, performing, and giving their best at all times, then the manager's employee file becomes irrelevant.

When a member of the workforce disregards managerial direction and violates the trust and confidence of the manager and the rest of the team, actual physical documentation and file management becomes necessary. Effective documentation is one of the many steps a professional manager must take to be effective when the need for discipline exists.

Treat your employees the way in which you wish to be treated and see things from their perspective. When you make this leap as a manager you have stepped into the fold of not just being a manager but becoming a great manager and leader among your workgroup.

Chapter 7 – Win with Positive Reinforcement

As managers, we set the tone and create the culture of our departments and organizations by our actions and our examples. We can create a work environment that is conducive to employee motivation and innovation, higher productivity and job satisfaction, higher morale and less turnover, all through some simple and basic tools that are at our immediate disposal. Developing a positive culture comes from actively seeking positive reinforcement and engaging in the appropriate managerial behavior using prescribed methods.

Positive Reinforcement

Positive reinforcement is the act of a manager engaging in "Good Finding." This means catching employees doing good things and thanking them for their performance. The guidelines for delivering positive reinforcement are:

- ✓ Personalized
- ✓ Immediate
- ✓ Frequent (ideally 7 to 1 but at least 4 to 1 ratio of positive versus corrective)
- ✓ Sincere
- ✓ Separated from Punishment
- ✓ Separated from Goal Setting
- ✓ Specific
- ✓ Systematized

When you provide positive reinforcement, you must keep it:

- ✓ Sincere
- ✓ Specific
- ✓ Immediate
- ✓ Personal

The frequency in which you provide positive reinforcement will vary based upon where you are at in the process of shaping behavior with an individual, and with a group overall. When you first start out you may need to make sure that reinforcement is frequent and regular to begin the shaping process. Continuing for too long at a regular interval can cause your reinforcement to reach a saturation point and behavior modification and shaping will stop. There is no magic number of days or weeks that you can apply to this and it may vary from one person to another. Use your managerial instincts to decide when it is appropriate to start modifying the frequency and move toward an intermittent approach. When handled properly, positive reinforcement intervals can become further apart and random in occurrence while still maintaining the desired behavioral changes. A fundamental rule of positive reinforcement is that once it is started and used effectively, it cannot stop!

As humans we respond to stimuli that make us feel good about ourselves. We also respond to a reward that we receive for doing something well. As a result, we tend to change our behavior to try and receive more of the things that we like and want by engaging in more of the behavior that we know will give us the desired reward. Fishing is one example of this. When a person starts to fish for the first time, it helps that they are able to catch fish. To get the person to want to fish more it helps that they are able to catch a fish fairly often which drives them to engage in the behavior even more. If at the initial stages of fishing they stop catching fish altogether, they will likely choose a different hobby. If they in turn catch a fish every time they cast, over a long enough period of time they will get bored with the activity and probably choose a different hobby. However, catching fish and especially catching the larger trophy fish requires diligence and determination, honing of skills and better preparation, and therefore more engagement in fishing behavior with a periodic reward of a nice sized fish. Not knowing when and where for sure that big fish will be caught, only knowing that the big fish is there somewhere and periodically will be on the end of their hook will drive a person to fish even more. The excitement of catching that random large fish carries a person through hours, and weeks, and months, sometimes years of drought because of the reward it brings them.

The same is true of positive recognition that we receive at work from our managers. When properly done, a workforce will overachieve on a consistent basis and find happiness in their efforts and results because they are recognized for their contribution.

Let's go back to the fishing example for a minute. How does the fishing example relate to the catalog of eight principles listed above?

1. Personalized – it is me catching the fish.
2. Immediate – I do not find out later about having caught a fish, I know immediately when I set the hook.
3. Frequent (ideally 7 to 1 but at least 4 to 1 ratio of positive versus corrective) – as long as I do not get

snagged or in trouble fishing more than once every 4 to 7 fish I am okay.

4. Sincere – the fish are not kidding me; they actually bite the lure intentionally because they want to.
5. Separated from Punishment – I am not provided a fish to make me feel better about a snag; however, I have been surprised to catch a fish when I thought I had a snag!
6. Separated from Goal Setting – Whether I establish that I am not going to be happy unless I catch x number of fish, the act of catching fish in general makes me happy.
7. Specific – the fish biting my lure is the specific reward assuming I can get it in the net; if I do then I can likely determine that a specific technique I used made a difference in the outcome.
8. Systematized – there is a system and process I need to follow to catch fish from how deep and far to cast, what bait to use, etc.

There are many behaviors that we as humans engage in that provide reinforcement for our efforts and shape our actions and who we are. Some of them are problematic like alcoholism, gambling, stealing, overeating, watching too much TV, wasteful spending, reckless driving, etc. Some are less damaging yet still problematic like following a leader who is not genuine, radical activity against a good establishment, supportive behavior toward a bad establishment, sarcasm, self oppression, arrogance, etc.

What we as managers want to do is create an environment where doing the right things to support the well being of the workforce helps us achieve company objectives. Also, where the activities and employee behavior that will lead us to these accomplishments gets properly recognized and reinforced so that we are not only able to hit our goals but maintain future prosperity and growth through our team's actions.

Seems simple; it all starts with you and how you recognize your people.

Correcting Behavior

Okay, people may claim that it is easy to give employees good news, but a real manager is the one who can confront conflict and deliver the tough messages! There is no doubt that you will need to provide difficult and challenging news to your employees at some point in your managerial career. There should never be a tally of the number of employees you have terminated as if stickers on the back of your football helmet. Having fired a lot of people or not having had to fire a lot of people should never determine whether you are a good or bad manager. The fact is at some point you will face a situation where you need to deliver bad news whether it is through a termination, a layoff, a plant closing, etc. The most effective way to manage through a situation like this is to be well grounded on your use of performance management and employee recognition.

Positive recognition expertise provides the base for you to leverage to effectively correct and shape behavior in a way that is impactful and respected by the employee or employees affected. Can you make a bad situation into a positive one? Remember our theme: problems beget profits. As a professional manager you can improve behavior in a positive way; you can even manage a termination in a way that ends up becoming a positive experience for the person affected.

The guidelines to follow when correcting performance utilizing the techniques discussed above are:

1. Always specify the performance being corrected
2. Use data to:
    a. Build a case for improvement, not for dismissal
    b. Focus correction on performance, not the performer
    c. Confirm that a consequence is a punisher

3. Provide reinforcement for the desired performance (Ideally an incompatible performance)
    a. This is the most important guideline!

4. Correct immediately
5. Don't correct when angry
6. Be consistent
7. Maintain a ratio of 4 to 1; (ideally 7 to 1)
8. Do not use the sandwich method
    a. Telling someone that they are doing well at something to soften the blow, and then telling them that they need to improve something, then ending with a comment that they are doing good. Doing this simply confuses the person and you lose the impact of what you are trying to convey regarding the employee behavior you wish to correct as a manager.

9. Never correct publicly

a.   However, it is great to provide positive reinforcement to someone in a public setting, if done properly it can be very powerful.

Consequences

There are four basic types of consequences; two of which work to increase behavior while the other two work to decrease behavior.

Consequences that increase behavior are:

- ➢ Positive reinforcement – giving the employee something that they want
- ➢ Negative reinforcement – taking away something from the employee that they don't want
   - a.   Removing a barrier from an employee to make them more productive is an example of this

Consequences that decrease performance are:

- ➢ Punishment – giving the employee something they don't want
- ➢ Extinction – taking away something that the employee wants

By far the most successful approach to changing employee behavior is through positive reinforcement. Not only will positive reinforcement change behavior in a more pleasing manner it has the power to maintain a higher level of performance and sustain that level of performance over time versus the use of other types of consequences.

A good example of this is with a person who has a behavior of speeding when they drive their car. In the world, as it is today, occasionally the speeder gets caught by radar and receives a citation that costs money and punishes them for their speeding behavior. In another world, if it may exist, what if occasionally a person gets caught going through radar and gets pulled over for driving the speed limit and the officer gives them a check for $100. This is definitely positive reinforcement at work.

In world "A", as it is today, the person with the speeding behavior will still speed when they can but they may develop another behavior of making sure they look closer for radar and may slow down in the same spot they originally got caught, but for the most part they will still speed. In an ideal world "B", a person may actually modify their behavior over time to try and get caught driving the speed limit as much as possible and especially if they continue to receive a random surprise of $100 for doing what they should be doing in the first place.

Positive Reinforcement is Free

The best positive reinforcement available to you is simple and costs nothing. Observing your people and letting them know that you appreciate something they have done is very powerful as long as it is done properly based on the guidelines mentioned previously. If you are making it too obvious that you are on a positive reinforcement mission and that you must provide a certain number of reinforcements to be competent as a manger you have probably already failed. If in the eyes of your employees you are truly sincere and demonstrate that you truly care about them as individuals then you are on the right path. Just taking time to smile and say good morning, use the employee's first name, take time to listen to them and be willing to engage in a conversation with them about their family or their thoughts and ideas on a subject. All these simple actions serve as powerful methods of providing positive reinforcement and recognition to your employees.

Remember you as a professional manager set the tone. Always display a positive attitude and exude consistent and affirmative emotional behavior around your employees. When you engage in an imbalance of emotional reactions and responses you put your employees on the edge and threaten their sense of security. The average employee ranks job security, a sense of belonging, and acceptance within the organization higher than any other criteria including salary. Knowing this a manager must always display confidence versus doubt in employee ability and department direction; encouragement versus fear in supporting and coaching an employee to achieve desired results; and trust versus mistrust in the manager/employee relationship. All of this can be achieved through positive recognition and reinforcement.

Spending money to provide a material reward can serve a purpose in shaping and reinforcing behavior but is best left to team initiatives to hit a team goal or reserved for special over-and-above situations that the team is facing in the business. Too much monetary recognition can become stale and can start to be viewed as an entitlement that the employees may expect to receive periodically and if they don't, it becomes non-motivating.

Remember to treat your employees the way in which you wish to be treated and see things from their perspective.

When you make this leap as a manager you have stepped into the fold of not just being a manager but becoming a great manager and leader among your workgroup.

To understand conflict is to understand life.

Chapter 8 – Understand Conflict

Conflict Resolution

Conflict resolution is a basic function of management. Whenever two or more people are engaged in an activity the possibility of conflict exists. Because our human tendency is to do things in a certain way our thoughts may not always agree with each other when more than one person is involved. It is simple to understand why . . . it is all based on our unique personal traits, upbringing, environment, and life experiences. Because of the innate and unique nature of human existence there will never be two people who think and act in the exact same manner in every situation. Periodic conflict will exist even in the most harmonious organizations and work environments. I once had exposure to a disconcerting situation whereby the training team responsible for basic supervisory and management skill development struggled with conflict and management values within their human resource department. That always left me puzzled; how could the team that was responsible for training management on basic management skills be themselves inept at management within their own team?

The key to dealing with conflict is resolution. Remember our basic premise in the book: problems beget profits. Conflict within the organization presents an opportunity for the professional manager to drive improvement. Without conflict there is no need for resolution. Without resolution there is no need to evaluate differences and identify solutions and therefore, there is no impetus for change. Conflict is a naturally occurring event in any human organization. Because of that fact conflict provides the basis for continuous improvement and growth. Problems beget profits because resolution is required; resolution represents the fuel that powers change in an organization. On the flipside problems left unresolved just as conflict not handled appropriately can have destructive effects on the organization.

There are many ways that conflict is dealt with in an organization. Interpersonal issues and problems between people may be addressed through attempts to suppress, to ignore (or non-attention), or with resolution. Of these three the only effective way to approach conflict is through resolution.

When no attempt is made by the manager to deal directly with a conflict situation there never is effective managerial resolution. Ignoring or denying attention to the issue leaves the conflict on its own to either be informally resolved by the parties involved, or as most often happens, left to fester into a destructive force within the workgroup.

Suppression of conflict is a harmful approach for a manager to take. This approach may reduce the outward negative consequences associated with a conflict situation, but it falls short of eliminating the root causes of the problem. In this shallow approach the manager fails to address or resolve the core issue and allows the reasons for the initial problem to persist as an antecedent condition for future problems.

When reasons, whether psychological, real, perceived, tangible, or emotional, that substantiate a conflict are eliminated, then conflict resolution is achieved. When true resolution is achieved all remnants of the original issue dissipate leaving the organization to move forward devoid of potential for antagonisms that could manifest into future conflicts.

There are various articles and books published regarding strategies to address conflict. Here conflict management strategies are categorized into three distinct groups: lose-lose, win-lose, and win-win. There is only one strategy proven to work; only when win-win is used will conflict resolution truly occur.

Lose-Lose Conflict

The worst approach used by a manager is one that results in a lose-lose outcome. Attempts to manage conflict by using compromise, smoothing or avoidance result in lose-lose consequences. In all three of these approaches neither party accomplishes their objectives or wishes. The conflict never gets resolved and the underlying reasons for the original problem remain embedded in the environment so that future conflicts of the same type will reoccur.

An obvious failed strategy that managers engage in is to avoid the conflict. Avoidance is a form of non-attention or ignorance at a severe level. The manager pretends that the conflict doesn't exist and just wishes it would go away. The manager thinks that the easiest way to deal with the problem is to avoid it and although initially it may actually seem like a path of least resistance; in the end it is the path that creates the greatest hardship and work for the manager and organization.

Normalizing the differences between people in an attempt to smooth out the rough edges and make things feel better creates a false level of true improvement. When a manager plays down the differences and emphasizes similarities and areas where the parties agree they are attempting to obtain peaceful co-existence. On the surface it seems like driving the conflict issue to recognition of the parties to common interests is a responsible goal. The problem with this strategy is the skipping over of the core issues of the initial conflict leaving them smoldering for future flame versus extinguishing them completely through true resolution.

One of the worst approaches management can use with the workforce is unfortunately widely accepted as a method for negotiating improvements in employee or labor relation situations. Compromise is the basic theme of labor union and management negotiations when dealing with issues that they are opposed to each other on regarding the work environment. Beyond the labor setting we find people generally working to a point of compromise in their relationships whether through community organizations, families, or work environments.

You may be wondering why compromise is an ineffective method of dealing with conflict. Compromise is the process of both parties relinquishing something of value to the other. Accommodating the process of compromise will result in neither party achieving its goals or desires. Although on the surface it may appear that the conflict has been resolved, unless the root issues are dealt with through true resolution the antecedent conditions that existed originally will still be present waiting for a future opportunity to surface and result in on-going conflict.

Win-Lose Conflict

Management and mankind in general will sometimes work to gain the upper hand at the expense or detriment of another person or group. In win-lose conflict desires of one party are gained only at the expense of the other party being excluded or denied their objectives or wishes in the relationship. In a competitive environment one team or individual will win, the other or others will lose.

Managers who pit one person or team against another in a manner that generates divergence will never achieve overall group acceptance by forcing a victor in a conflict situation. Here brute force, superiority, intimidation, or domination of one person or group over another is used to determine the outcome of a conflict situation. The same is true of a manager who uses authoritative command as a means of managing people. The dictator type manager decrees the solution and outcome dictating who gets what, who will win and who will lose, who gets what and who loses what. This format is basically easy to predict especially when the dictator is a party to the conflict.

All the above strategies work to suppress desires for some while rewarding others unconditionally. The end result is a lingering desire to achieve by some what they have been denied while at the same time creating dissatisfaction for the employees who realize they may never get fair consideration for their issues or concerns. Just like "lose-lose" strategies discussed in the previous section; the win-lose strategies also promote future conflict over the same issues. It is guaranteed that these conflicts will continue to surface or remain present within the workforce in the future.

Win-Win Conflict

The only strategy that eliminates conflict is resolution based on effective confrontation. Win-win conflict resolution can be achieved when problem solving techniques are used through confrontation of the issues and reconciliation of differences. When all parties involved in a conflict recognize that there is a problem to be solved, that something is wrong and needs changed or fixed, and that they are a party to the issue, then reconciliation and resolution can start to take shape. The manager must work through the facts surrounding the issue with a focus on the business and not the person or people involved in a positive and problem-solving fashion. Using this approach, the manager will find success with the results being a feeling of resolution by both parties. When the manager uses this approach then the conflict is truly resolved.

Once a win-win solution has been implemented then the reasons for the original conflict disappear and the new conditions ensure that no future conflict will surface as there will be nothing suppressed, avoided, smoothed over, or denied for one or both parties of the conflict. If the manager effectively opens up the issues to both parties in a fashion that allows both parties to ask for a solution that achieves both parties' desires and when both parties then agree or accept the solutions generated through the process then the win-win strategy is obtained. The win-win environment is created by the manager who gets his/her team to understand their collective obligation and desire to openly and honestly discuss feelings, thoughts, ideas, opinions, facts, and suggestions to drive improvement and resolve issues. Problems beget profits when the manager leads his/her people to understand that it is okay to discuss conflict situations and strive to resolve issues to get everyone to a better place and for the betterment of all involved in the organization.

Experts have indicated through their research that problem-solving combined with positive confrontation methods represents the most successful approach to conflict resolution. When people hold themselves accountable to the comments and actions they engage in, to dwell on the facts and truth of a situation and to the betterment and respect of the entire workgroup, the organization is positioned for success. A professional manager will automatically move toward positive and effective confrontation methods and will feel it awkward to consider competitive, autocratic, avoidance, smoothing, or compromise approaches to deal with a conflict situation. Companies and organizations that use confrontation and problem-solving techniques effectively will tend to out-perform those that do not.

Difficulty means you have more work to do – roll up your sleeves and dig harder - the rock in the way will not move itself.

Chapter 9 – Team Conflict and Difficult Conversations

Key Principles of Difficult Conversations

It's one thing when there is conflict or confusion between two people but when there is added problems created by fractured or ineffective communications a problem situation can become a challenging and difficult event. There has been much said about the importance of good communication in an organization. A professional manager must be a good communicator. Along with all the many things that a manager must engage in to lead their team to success communication is one of the top items on the list. Effective communication is something that cannot just be done right once and then abandoned, it must always be performed well for the manager to stay in the game.

There are some key principles that a manager must follow to deal effectively with difficult conversations. In all cases between two people there are two stories or two sides to a story. Messages get filtered by both parties involved in a conversation and that can lead to misunderstanding. A problem can occur due to the perception of both parties to the interpretation of the story.

Everyone anticipates the message as they receive it and predetermine the impact before the sender even has a chance to deliver it. This in itself can be a problem. A problem can be defined as the difference in the perception between the stories sent and received.

Think through the filters that people apply when speaking and listening to each other. The sender will filter the message they intend to deliver. The receiver will filter what they hear. Both filters influence the actual impact of the message. As a manager you must adjust the conversation and unbundle the facts to take control of the story. You must make reference to examples of the stories and demonstrate through the examples how they differ. You need to speak to and share perceptions, interpretations, and also principles related to the conversation. In all cases you must regulate the problem and redefine the conversation to get to the heart of the message. Continue in the process in a thoughtful and positive manner striving to point out the differences between the sent and received stories so that the message can be easily determined by all parties.

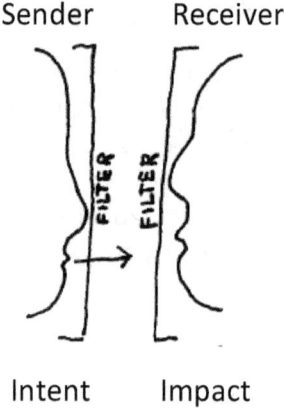

Sender   Receiver

FILTER   FILTER

Intent   Impact

Remember we all insert mental filters when speaking to each other. Just like putting on ear plugs in an airplane to reduce the sound coming from the plane and the other passengers, we apply filters or plugs to reduce distractions and maintain our present thoughts. In some cases the filters are used to minimize the message coming from the other person. There are many reasons for this; one is that we struggle to provide undivided attention to another in the midst of a high paced work environment where there is no time between meetings, conference calls, and deadlines. Another reason is that we apply a filter in anticipation of hearing a message that we would rather not hear, such as bad news, a negative report, or individual criticism.

To open up the filters and approach the communication in a constructive way start by not assuming negative intent or character. Adjust the communication to assume the best by giving benefit of doubt to the other person. As you open up your approach to the communication process you will create an environment for clearer understanding and sharing of thoughts and concerns. You will have moved the messaging process to a condition better suited to collaboration and resolution.

In all cases, change the approach from a position of affixing blame to a position of fact finding and assessment of individual involvement. The most important aspect of this portion of the communication process is perspective. In all cases you need to use perspective. It is always best for you to put yourself in the other person's shoes. By doing this you are encouraging and setting the example for others to do the same. Your most important task is to identify the individual involvement and contributions of each person to the given situation and work to help everyone grasp the individual perspectives and relationships.

It is helpful to view the situation from the perspective of a disinterested observer as another way of analyzing the issue. This of course does not mean to become disinterested in the issue; rather it will help you see the interaction from a different perspective. This will help you see yourself more as how the other person may be viewing you which will help you manage your approach and your choice of words and tone of voice.

I worked for a boss once who had a short attention span. He would make eye contact and listen when I was able to get time with him however he would turn away from me while I was speaking to him and act like he had something more important to do. I never felt like he ever understood anything I told him. To make matters worse, he cut short any conversation that involved details or collaborative discussion. In situations where it was important that he understood something about a difficult situation or project I felt smitten and left to believe that he was superior to both me and the issue. Mostly I was made to feel that what I was doing was not important. I also felt like I was not important to him either.

I imagined how this boss would feel if his boss did that to him. Later on I found out that not only did his boss do that to him, but his boss's boss did it also! What a chain of destructive communication that short circuited critical messages and involvement through necessary channels in the organization. Ineffective messaging and filtering can leave a company disconnected from the top to the bottom through something as simple as basic verbal and non-verbal messaging!

How much do we realize and appreciate the value of non-verbal messages? It is critical that you effectively position your feelings in a way that supports the message you are sending as well as your openness to receiving. It is okay to have feelings; acknowledge and express them appropriately. In difficult situations it is the feelings more than the words conveyed that make a difference. To manage the communication process, you must adjust the pretense using effective emotional behavior. Premeditated and well rehearsed emotional behavior can be very effective. It is better to perform with emotion instead of being emotional.

Remember as a manager in the workplace, "Emotions have no brains." Negative emotion must be avoided, overall emotion must be kept in-check, and positive emotion can be uplifting and highly motivational when handled properly.

As a manager you absolutely must understand and recognize conflict as a threat to an employee's security in their job and a serious threat to the sense that they have of who they are. The most important attributes on the average person's list touch on personal security and sense of belonging. When it comes to the assessment of their job and their performance employees will be concerned about several areas or central identities. These innermost identities are constantly being reviewed in the employees' minds throughout their workday, albeit both subconsciously and consciously they are the pillars with which an employee finds security in their work existence.

Deep inside a person is always asking themselves if they are viewed by others as being capable and competent. People need to feel that others view them as good at what they do and basically thought of as a good person. The cords of this innermost identity run deep into the thoughts a person has about whether they are worthy of care and concern from others. All people want others to love them and care about them as a person.

Any shock to the central identities and a situation can be thrown off balance. Maintaining balance is critical and must be an on-going effort. Once central identities are threatened, it may be very hard if not impossible to bring things back into balance. To improve your ability to recognize and cope with identity issues when they hit: be sensitive to the other person's needs, be aware of your own identity issues as a manager, decipher both your own and the other person's identity complexities, think through and anticipate responses before delivering a message, and position yourself to receive a message using active listening.

Active Listening

In all conflict situations and as a general rule of managerial conduct you need to turn on active listening to be successful. It is helpful to follow the pattern below to ensure that you are hearing and demonstrating active listening in a conflict situation.

How many times have you simply wished that you had someone to talk to about an issue or concern? Generally it is not when you are satisfied or content. It is usually when you are upset about something that has happened to you or when you feel like someone has mistreated you that you reach out to a peer or a friend to consult with. When someone approaches you on an issue they have trusted that the relationship they have with you is a strong and personal one. As a manager you want your people to feel comfortable coming to you when they are troubled. Showing concern and respect for them and the position they have regarding an issue is important to supporting them in the process. Active listening means you engage as a facilitator and release valve for the employee to regain their balance and place.

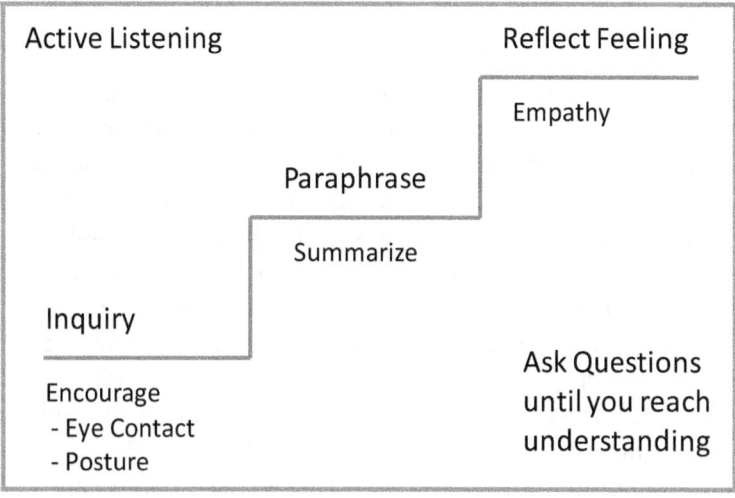

I am reminded of the following poem entitled *Listening* as it relates to the human condition and the deep need that we all have for someone to listen to us especially when we are struggling with a difficult situation:

> *Can we share our story with others, will it settle our mind?*
> *Finding peace in the midst of battle; separating oneself from the rest of mankind.*
> *Listening to one's sharing when there is no one else there.*

Listening is a form of speaking telling another that you care.
A plant can shoot upward through the hard, frozen, ground. By being present you can help someone through a hardship, without making a sound.

I can still remember one of my first bosses who would sit up straight when I entered his office. He would set his pad of paper to the left side of his desk along with his pencil, stop anything he was doing at the time, and focus 100% of his attention on me. He made direct eye contact and maintained a non-verbal composure that welcomed my comments and showed concern for what I was saying. He always ended the conversation by paraphrasing back what I said and discussed with me possible solutions. He took notes of the key items that he felt important while I was speaking. He maintained eye contact and showed genuine concern for me. In future discussions he shared with me the status of any concern or thought that I had previously shared with him.
He expected the same respect from me and others when meeting with him. To enter his office unprepared and disconnected from the discussion left the person on the other side of his desk melting under the direct yet respectful critique that he provided the violator – very effective!

Maintain Balance

Even as a professional manager you must understand and accept certain things about yourself and your involvement when dealing with a conflict situation. The first thing to understand is that you may have contributed to the problem by virtue of your involvement, but you are also the vehicle of resolution. Your intentions may also be complex especially if the situation is complex; do not be set back by the complexity of conflict, rather accept it and prepare yourself to move forward. Most importantly you must understand that you will make mistakes, everyone does, remember we are all human.

Acknowledge your mistakes quickly if things get out of balance. Become good at moving forward with an issue and conversation by picking up in an area where the parties may find a non-threatening and positive direction. It may take some time and experience but admit to being unpolished and human. Whatever you do avoid making excuses. Your job as a professional manager is to find the right balance and maintain a productive exchange of information to achieve a target, build an interpersonal relationship, satisfy an employee need, and accomplish a business objective.

Use the experience of others who have gone before and performed well at balancing communications. Do not attempt to control the other person's emotions and reaction. Anticipate and plan in advance for possible reactions. Think beyond the present to a place in the future to help put the current issue in a broader perspective. How will this issue be viewed in terms of its overall importance next month, next year, or five years from now? Pace the process to allow time to think and prepare. Do not feel like everything must be resolved in the first session, in a hurry, or immediately. Take time to breathe and think and allow the other person the same break in the action. Overall communication will achieve a greater level of relevance and engagement if dosed out and consumed properly.

Managers make mistakes many times in dealing with a conflict situation. There are a few key things you should avoid at all costs as a manager. The first is assuming as a manager that you are right, and the other person is wrong. Next failure point is when perspective is missing – a shortage of questions can derail any conversation. A manager must be open to seeing things from multiple and different angles to get the best overall view of the true situation. It is critical that you see how the other person views the situation before proceeding. Finally recognize that squelching emotions and burying feelings is not an effective method of resolving conflict. Staying rational and repressing emotions should not be a purpose of the manager in these situations. That line of thought does not contribute to effective problem solving.

A manager must use a few key steps in handling difficult conversations to be effective. First: use forward thinking and know your purpose and what you hope to accomplish. Next: prepare for the most difficult response and outcome in advance. Think through the back and forth discussion and be honest about what you feel will knock you off course, so you can acknowledge it and have a plan for dealing with it if it does happen. Finally: be open and honest, be yourself. Do not try to be someone you are not. There is no need for eloquence, no place for arrogance, and no point in manipulating the message and situation to something other than what it really is. Call it as you see it but be open to and take ownership to the situation yourself.

Emotional Discipline

A common myth is that we believe events are the reason we feel the way we feel. In actuality it is not the event; it is our interpretation of the event. Because of this it is important as a manager to change the way you think in order to change the way you feel and act. View the process as follows: Event;

Interpretation; Reaction; Behavior. It may help if you think about this from a primal perspective. Instinctively we humans rely on emotions for basic survival. A lion in the bush adjacent to your campsite may demonstrate the sequence of emotional release. You hear a growl or mild roar rumbling through the leaves just a few feet away from you. You grab for your spear as the lion steps forward from the bush into the grass wrinkling nostrils and showing long sharp teeth below the upper snout. Your immediate interpretation is the lion is hungry and wants to eat you! Your reaction is sheer panic and horrific thoughts race through your mind as you see yourself dying a horrible death. Your instinctive behavior is to run as fast as you can and hope that somehow you can outrun the lion! What other choice do you have – the wooden spear with a stone tip?

It is amazing how often we act in the same fight or flight manner today over situations that are not life-threatening. We have engrained inside us the feeling of horror when we see a lion not because of the lion sighting but because of our reaction to the event and our thoughts about what could happen to us. We have an instinct driven by emotion when faced with a problem or difficult situation.

We touched on something similar when we discussed core identities; now let's look at three basic human belief systems that control our interpretation of who we are as people, how we respond to ourselves, to others, and to the world in general. The first belief is what we believe to be true about ourselves. The second is what we believe to be true about others and how we believe they should treat us. Lastly what we believe about how the work environment, community, country, world, etc. is supposed to work.

As a manager you must know and understand different people's perspectives and belief systems. By doing this you will be better positioned to approach a situation and create a plan for successful resolution. Think about how you as a manager are reacting to the situation. Ask yourself: "How bad is it really?" Take stock of your own emotional behavior and how you feel about others and the environment. Are you under or overreacting to the situation? More than likely a manager's tendency will be to overreact.

What does my managerial face look like? Am I keeping my emotions in balance? Remember as a manager it is important to change the way you think to change the way you act. You must prepare for each situation in advance. Premeditate your behavior in some cases to be different than what you feel inside if the situation calls for it. Do not be afraid of change. If you open up to all possible perspectives in every situation you will not only train yourself to think differently but also change the way you feel and over time become a better manager as you develop a new normal response to conflict situations. I strongly believe that you must take on something new every day in your life to continue to grow and develop as a person. So too with your managerial ability you must always challenge yourself to new and different ways of behaving as a leader. Professional managers do not pay their dues only once; they pay them every day!

Here are a few points to consider in the process of changing behavior:

> Ask others for feedback on a regular basis; establish an environment of trust
> Seek to better understand
> Decide if it is a worthwhile effort to change

- How important is it that I prevail in the situation?
- Display a willingness to evaluate the change process
- Allocate time to preparation
- Allow time for introspection
- Write the behavior change down in an after-action log

Remember that changing behavior can be a slow and difficult process. At times it will feel like you are using a stone weapon to fight a lion. Our natural instinct is to react to change in a defensive manner to protect ourselves from attack or failure. If the lion is leaving me alone in my current situation, then why invite it into my campsite by changing things? A professional manager works through the list of key points to use when changing behavior with an employee recognizing that it takes time, persistence, and diligence. A professional manager does not give up but keeps repeating the key points to get to the end of the process.

Checklist for Successful Conflict Management

Conflict Management Checklist

- ✓ Ask open-ended questions
    - o   Use a low voice tone
    - o   Speak slowly, clearly and deliberately
    - o   Don't say too much
- ✓ Don't underestimate
- ✓ Don't make assumptions
- ✓ Ask: "How can I help?"
- ✓ Know the person's hot button
- ✓ Know the person's skill level in conflict situations
- ✓ Understand where the emotion is coming from
- ✓ Let the person vent privately
    - o   Manager must take charge of situation
    - o   Stop the conversation and take it to a private setting
- ✓ Use alternate self-talk approach
- ✓ Take all egos out of it; focus on empathy for the person
- ✓ Refrain from point/counterpoint responses
- ✓ Control your non-verbal responses
- ✓ Put yourself in a mediator role; focus on asking questions

To attract fish to follow use a leader to pull the lure; to achieve an objective tie leadership to the front of the line.

Chapter 10 – Team Leadership

Leadership Basics

There are numerous books and articles written about leadership. A professional manager is an effective leader that abides by the principles of basic management techniques. Using these techniques, a professional manager leads their team to positive results. Leadership is synonymous with control, direction, guidance, and management. Professional leadership is in essence professional management. There are certain aspects of leadership that are worth mentioning to ground a manager on basic principles that take them from having a manager title to becoming a true leader. This section helps make those distinctions and provides the understanding necessary for managerial development.

Leaders are rarely named or appointed. People follow other people for a reason; not because a person has been given a title or a name. Certainly there have been exceptions to this throughout history; however, Marie Antoinette may disagree today if she could about the value of a name or title when your neck is on the line! People follow people for many reasons and because they do, we have leaders. Leaders are people that get others to follow them. In some cases, the leader does not actually want people to follow them but because of something they did or said, or because a situation they have been caught up in creates visibility to them, they end up with people following them or following a perception of them.

Later in this chapter we will discuss key attributes of a leader and how they are important. All leaders share a sense of responsibility to something, a degree of competence to a subject, passion and an ability to communicate in an effective way, a standard that they believe in, a connection and understanding of what people want, and a vision or plan for the future that they are promoting to get others to subscribe to. It is important to note that not all leaders are leading people to do good things. In too many cases people are led to follow a person who incites evil and inflicts pain or damage on other groups of people. Hitler was a brilliant leader but a terrible and horrific human being! History is littered with people following the wrong people for the wrong reasons. What we will discuss is the attributes that are needed to ensure that you will become a good leader in pursuing your career as a positive and effective professional manager.

Welcome to the staff meeting and to the company's management team! Now that you have the word manager in your title you have the official capacity to become a leader. That is you are now a company recognized leader on the formal management team. You may have been a hard worker before and earned your promotion because of your dedication and contributions to the organization. I hope you earned a manager title due to the managerial competencies that your management team recognized in you and may have worked with you to develop to prepare you for the job. You may have already been a very effective informal leader in your workgroup. Now it is time to learn more about expanding your leadership skills to become a professional manager.

Let's start with lesson number one: being a member of the company's management team does not make you a leader! It does give you the opportunity to earn the respect of the employees who report to you and earn the right to lead them. You cannot be promoted to a leader, the right to lead people is granted to you by the people that you lead. Your promotion to a leadership role gives you the formal authority but make no mistake about it, the promotion does not give you the power to lead people.

Why? Because people detest being managed! People prefer to be led. People are instinctively looking for someone to follow who will provide them something they can feel better about or relate to. Many times people will follow a person in the hope that the person will lead them to a better life. Whether you create an environment conducive to people being interested in following you is totally up to you and your ability to be an effective leader. This is parallel to your ability to be a professional manager. Remember people will always follow someone else in an organization, the question is: are they following you and doing the things that you need them to do to accomplish the organization's objectives.

Many managers start out on the path of holding people accountable and forcing their compliance to a system or a process. If you are struggling as a leader it could be that your people feel like they are being managed and not led. Micro-management exists because inexperienced managers have a basic lack of understanding and a corresponding insecurity surrounding the people and the work that they are responsible for managing. Because they lack basic knowledge of the work being done and they are weak in their management skill level they resort to micro-managing their people to make sure that as a manager they can speak to and be held accountable for the work being done.

Nothing infuriates a workforce more than a boss who doesn't know what they are doing standing over their shoulders forcing an explanation of everything that gets done! The leadership that develops out of this environment forces the employees to follow anyone (other than their manager) who will relieve them of this oppression. Many times we see labor union organization occurring, high turnover, or attendance and attitude issues coming from the group afflicted. Overall department performance generally suffers in this situation. The people being micro-managed always seem to feel like they are overworked and need more help.

Whatever you do as a manager do not get caught up in having people merely obey you because you have the authority to order them to do something. Your people will do the bare minimum to get by and will not support you. If you have exceptional people who work hard and generate significant results through their own desire and intrinsic reward system you will be the beneficiary of the results achieved by these people, but you will not be the reason for the improvements. To the hard working and self-achieving people in your department you will be viewed as an obstacle that they need to overcome to achieve results in spite of you!

On the contrary, when people feel like they are truly being led they will run through brick walls to get things done for you. Our human spirit to compete, build, create, accomplish, receive recognition and feel good about who we are as physical beings is very strong. A professional manager will inspire and spark the spirit inside people to do things beyond the workgroup's functional requirements. A strong leader will get people to perform well beyond their job descriptions. People committed to their manager will follow them well past the manager's formal level of authority also. Remember people will commit to a leader before they commit to a company or organization. People tend to leave companies because of their manager and not because of the company.

Leadership comes down to trust. People will not follow someone they do not trust. Trust is earned daily by the professional manager. You must follow proper guidelines to be a professional manager and you must follow the lead from the people you represent and support.

> *To lead you must follow, to follow you must lead.*
> *For to lead people on the right path, you must follow*
> *the right way.*

Ultimately your task is to make a difference in the organization but more importantly, to make a difference in the lives of the people you work with. Leaders make a difference - everyday!

Leadership Characteristics

The characteristics of a professional manager and a strong leader are important to recognize. These key characteristics are what influence employees to behave in a certain way. There are numerous ways that a leader can adopt an effective style of leadership; all are acceptable as long as they maintain a balance between consideration for the employee as an individual and the needs of the company or organization.

A strong leader has a strong sense of personal and professional responsibility. They demonstrate their leadership by putting the needs of others first. They also demonstrate self-control in everything they do. In particular they are under control when things become difficult or challenging. They do not hit the panic button every time they think there could be a problem. In fact, they don't own a panic button let alone use it. They also maintain control of their personal lives. If there are personal issues, they are not surfaced at work. The leader will do the things that others feel they should in upholding true leadership status. They promote the style and characteristics that other people desire. They also represent the individual that people strive to be more like. Because of this people will be attracted to the manager they feel best represents their ideals and will follow their chosen influential leader.

A strong leader will make good decisions. If they do not have all of the technical skills needed the employees will assist them in knowledge absorption for a period of time but in the end the manager must learn what they need to know to make the right decisions for the business or organization. Confiding in people in a way that engenders them and grants their support is important to a manager in building the required competence in the eyes of the employees.

Although some areas to a manager may be unfamiliar, they must press onward in a new direction to build their own experience in the subject area they are responsible for. Shirking or hiding from the unfamiliar will cause a manager to lose the respect of the workforce. A strong leader will approach new challenges and embark in new directions with enthusiasm, commitment, and a desire to put their own ego on a shelf while they work to support the team in the achievement of a new level of accomplishment. If the leader is involved in the work being done and is willing to share in the importance of that work, it is easier for employees to demonstrate pride in the work that they do. My boss knows what I do and appreciates what I do therefore I am proud of my work and more willing to do what my boss asks me to do.

You will rarely find a chapter on management that does not include communication skills. All forms of effective communication are critical to the success of a leader. Listening and hearing what employees are saying is important. Messages are interpreted and evaluated without personal bias or opinion by the leader who makes a positive difference in the organization. A strong leader is disciplined in their listening skills. The overall ability of a manager to communicate effectively pulls the workgroup together and holds them together through the challenges and opportunities they face.

A strong value system and a high standard of personal conduct and professional ethics are at the core of group interaction, decision-making quality, and employee acceptance. The key ingredient is the employee's ability to rely on the actions of their manager. Well-established value systems that have been proven to survive over time and over a variety of challenging situations create the backdrop necessary for the manager to become an effective leader. A professional manager puts the interests of their employees and organization ahead of their individual pride even when their senior manager may not. Demonstrating a high level of integrity and ethical standards helps the professional manager maintain their conditioning and their place in the world of accomplished managers with the capacity to lead people effectively. Regardless of the team you are playing for you want to be the best at the position you have trained hard for and worked to earn.

Create a Positive Environment

Does a manager motivate the workforce? Does a great leader motivate people to follow them because they behave in a prescribed manner? I contend that no single person can motivate another person. As much as you would like to think that you can change someone else the reality is you can only change one person, and that person is yourself. If a person wants to change it is because they have decided to change and not due to someone else changing them.

What a manager and leader can do is create an environment for change. Building a climate that is encouraging and supportive of change is something that great leaders and you as a professional manager must do to drive the organization forward. Employee motivation is all about creating an environment that allows and encourages people to motivate themselves to do something different.

A manager faces a sense of loss of control at times when they are not able to force people to change. You cannot force motivation! Giving people independence to act in a manner that connects them to the organization's goals and objectives because you as a manager have created an environment that supports and reinforces those behaviors is truly garnering managerial control although on the surface to those less experienced it appears like a loss of control! In soccer the coach encourages passing the ball to score. By giving up a low percentage shot or a one-on-one run to the net a forward can pass the ball off and give up control to another and by virtue of doing that the team may be more likely to score. In some situations, by giving up control and passing the ball to another forward you are more likely to get the ball back and be able to score. A Give-to-Get strategy works in soccer and it also works in managing people.

As a professional manager it is your responsibility to create a positive work environment. It takes skill and experience to do this. Managers who lack experience and confidence in the field they are engaged in will tend to hold things close for fear of not getting the work done right. Their tendency is to micromanage the workforce to keep the work inside their comfort zone due to their overall insecurity. As you might guess from the description provided this is not an acceptable method of developing and maintaining a healthy and positive work climate.

There is truth to the fact that the higher the academic/skill level required for the employee to perform in a position the more you should expect to see the employee demonstrating self initiative in their work behavior. However, it is wrong for you to treat people as if they are not responsible and/or expect that they cannot be. Putting it simply, if you as a manager must babysit the employees you have in order to get the job done, you have failed in your hiring decisions or you have not created a work environment conducive to employee self motivation.

Here are a few key areas of focus that can help you as a manager:

Manage by objectives. Do not spend your time telling people how to do the job, rather focus on providing them the tools and resources they need and give them a clear picture of the results you are looking to achieve. Leave the methods of getting the job done to the people you are assigning the work. Hold them accountable to the results not the methods used.

With that being said you must make sure that the methods used meet any critical company or organization guidelines for safety, ethics, proper accounting procedures, etc. and that the management of other employees in obtaining the results meets the guidelines expected of a professional manager.

Suggest methods do not dictate them. If you have trained your people properly and developed a positive work environment strategy you will appreciate and encourage people to devise solutions that may actually work better. Remember your job as a professional manager is not to come up with all of the answers. The best solutions and ideas for an organization to drive operational improvement generally come from the people doing the work.

Consult and confide in people. Always engage people in the development of a solution regardless of whether you think you need their input or not. One of the most meaningful ways of showing recognition to one of your employees is to confide in them regarding the business. Asking people their opinions and involving them in the discussions regarding a problem or plan for improvement is an effective way of managing change as you create a positive work culture.

Always find ways to enrich the work your people do in their day-to-day jobs. A professional manager delegates as far down the chain as possible and close to the point of impact to get the maximum engagement and involvement from the people who do the actual work. You are a manager not a worker, remember that. Your job is to get people to do what they might otherwise not do in a manner that excites and motivates them in a positive way to contribute to the success of the organization. Do not withhold training and exposure of business opportunities from your people because you think they might not be capable of more. Instead challenge people to go outside of their comfort zone. By doing this you are a party to assisting the employee in finding competencies that they might not otherwise realize inside themselves. This is fundamental to employee development. As a professional manager you must always be looking for ways to help a person develop their skills and careers.

Provide good guidance to your people. Set an example and encourage thought consistent with constructive suggestions that you have in mind for the department or company. If you engage your people in the process of coming up with suggestions and presenting them instead of you doing the presentation work yourself, you will be able to create a culture that rewards employee initiative and motivation.

Rules that are not important or needless should be eliminated. Give people freedom and mobility as long as they achieve the results you are looking for. You will know when you have given too much latitude as your employees may question the situation. Generally people will restrict themselves more than you will need to within the confines of what they feel safe and comfortable with. Guidelines must be provided and reinforced so that people do not interfere with other departments or people in their work.

As a professional manager you will never abdicate your responsibility, lose control of the situation, or fall short of achieving results if you follow the guidelines above. In addition, you will develop a work environment that drives for continuous results, innovates and maneuvers change in a positive way and attracts great talent as people will enjoy being a part of your team.

I learned a basic lesson on creating a positive work environment and maximizing results as a baseball coach. An experienced team manager and long-time coach taught me to ease the tension each batter faces before stepping into the batter's box by communicating positive messages before and after each turn at bat. He told me that a batter under pressure to perform will tense up their muscles holding their arms and elbows in close to the body and will invariably swing and miss the ball every time. When the batter relaxes and establishes presence inside their comfort zone within the batter's box, they are positioning their body to do well at what naturally they are capable of and conditioned to do. Invariably the batter in this mindset will swing the bat with confidence and hit the ball.

Build Credibility

A professional manager is always building; building their reputation, building relationships, developing processes, creating improvements, constructing alliances and bridges between groups and departments, creating an environment for people to motivate themselves to a higher level of productivity, and building their managerial credibility among the workgroup. Integrity and credibility are essential for a manager to be effective in accomplishing objectives. Achieving a high level of credibility is necessary for a manager not only with employees but with peers and senior managers.

A manager has managerial competencies to draw upon to build credibility such as being genuine in their actions and communications, demonstrating sincerity and concern for their team members, and setting the example for integrity and fairness. Trying to be something that they are not will cause a manager to fail. People see through the mask of a manager who tries to be someone they are not. People detest others who become managers and change their personality to be something different or to give the appearance of superiority because of their new title as manager.

The best thing a manager can do is to act as they really are. Facades crumble in the eyes of employees and hiding provides little refuge. If the manager has a bad personality and does not care for others to begin with, chances are they are going to fail as a manager anyway. A professional manager has a caring and understanding personality that people feel secure and comfortable with. The key is being yourself and being the person that your people will put their trust into as they put forth effort to help you achieve success for the team and the organization.

Sound simple? It is not! Why? A professional manager must always maintain a balance and do the right things for the right reasons. There are many areas to focus on to be successful in building credibility. The following areas are keys to this success:

Frank, open and honest behavior, basic candor and truthfulness all provide a foundation for building credibility. Speaking straightforward thoughts and expressing opinions and directives in objective and factual ways without the attempt to hide, cover up, manipulate, distort or hedge a position is important to a professional manager. Employees want to understand things better and appreciate the truth behind a situation. They feel a sense of trust from their manager if they are spoken to directly and engaged in the process of information exchange in a constructive manner. Facts overlooked or ignored only get the manager in trouble if they have not thought through the situation well or attempt to hide or exaggerate to accomplish an objective.

The world suffers from a lack of consistency in information. Telling one group one thing and then twisting the message around to tell another group something entirely different only serves to diminish the credibility of the manager. A professional manager is consistent in the way that they deal with people and consistent in the message they provide. They are consistent in the environment they create and can be relied on by their team members for a response that fits the mold of the culture they have created. Nothing shakes the security of an employee more than the unpredictable behavior of their manager. A professional manager knows this and makes sure that they are consistent in the way they interact with their people.

A professional manager also knows that they cannot treat everyone exactly the same. That is not the intent of being consistent. Knowing your people's needs and working to support them all in the ways that they need support and doing so consistently for everyone over time will provide the environment that drives productivity and satisfaction for the team. The manager has the lead role in making sure this happens within their workgroup.

We all know that a promise kept is a promise not broken. A professional manager proceeds thoughtfully when making promises to people. They contemplate what can be achieved with what might not be practical before making statements and getting people's hopes up. The key to a manager's credibility is their ability to act on the things they promise to people. Keeping promises is more about managerial action and results versus words and wishful thinking. That does not mean that a manager should not provide vision and take risks to drive change in an organization. It is all in the messaging that a manager portrays a promise of something better and a method for achieving it. Moses led his people into the desert to a better life free from affliction, but it took forty years to achieve the Promised Land. Making promises may not always mean that a manager can make things instantly better; rather it is sometimes the truth of the situation and the contingencies involved that must be effectively communicated so that people will believe and follow to a better place in the organization.

Being open and receptive to the people they are responsible for is a basic tenant of managerial credibility. Accessibility is a companion to credibility. People need to feel a part of the organization and their ability to communicate their thoughts, ideas, and concerns to the manager is critical in this engagement. A professional manager is not just accessible to their people but also receptive to them. Remember your number one job as a manager is to lead your people. When an employee approaches you with a question or concern it is your number one job to stop everything else you are doing and provide them your undivided attention. Nothing distances you more from your team than your impression of having something more important to do than listen to an employee who needs you.

A professional manager always uses "we" when describing success with an objective. They also use "I" when describing a shortcoming and avoid "we" or "they" when discussing difficulties. Accepting responsibility is important for a manager. It is the manager's responsibility to share positive and negative communication with their people. Hiding or blaming someone else when announcing an unpopular or difficult decision or message is not taking on the responsibility of a professional manager. How can a manager expect their employees to act responsible when they do not take on the responsibility they have as a manager? A professional manager who knows and does the job well will promote their personal and professional credibility.

Confidence and straightforward communication is important to a professional manager. Using a calm and well modulated voice displaying only positive emotion will provide the consistency and secure feeling of the people reporting to the manager. This calm and straightforward approach enhances credibility. It provides the assurance to others that things are hopeful, and the team is capable of accomplishing the task or objective.

Personal style and managerial personality is critical to a professional manager's success. A manager who harbors fear and doubt creates the impression among their employees that they are not doing the job and that their jobs may be at risk. Promoting doubt and fear by questioning everything and challenging everything in a negative or destructive manner can lead to a department unraveling at the seams.

A professional manager challenges people in a constructive and positive way showing coaching and support for alternative solutions or ideas and confiding in people to conclude methods of improvement. Supplanting ideas for improvement within the team and showing recognition for team member's realization of ideas will provide the best method of growing and cultivating positive change in the organization.

A professional manager will always ask employees to do something versus ordering and demanding that something get done. Employees wish to be treated with respect and when treated with respect they will generally act respectful. Consistent application of respect along with proper recognition for the employee's work is important in building credibility. A professional manager wants to make the employee feel included and important to the work they need to do instead of belittled and beleaguered.

A professional manager is interested in their employees, not only in the work they do but also in them as a person. Knowing a little about the employee's family or personal interests is important in building a credible relationship with them. That does not mean that you have a right or responsibility to meddle in their personal affairs or provide your opinion on personal matters. That crosses the line for the manager who needs to maintain a proper interest in their employees. Several skills are essential in demonstrating proper interest; attentive listening and patience are basics. A manager should not be expected to have all the answers. It is okay to tell people that you do not know the answer, but it is then your responsibility as a manager to find the answer and get back to the employee. This is another basic way of demonstrating interest in employees and goes a long way in building managerial credibility.

Building and maintaining credibility is important. It takes effort and persistence for a manager to succeed. A professional manager never stops working to build credibility. Credibility is not a one-time fee that is paid just as being a professional athlete requires constant training and conditioning, a manager must constantly hone his/her skills to be the best they can possibly be.

Emulate Model Management

What are some of the traits that you look for in finding a perfect leader or a model manager? What does it mean to be a top notched manager? If you think back to the people you have worked for or with, or people in the community or world who fit the description, how long is your list? Probably rather short!

To find a model manager you need to look for specific traits that set them apart from the rest of the pack. In many ways the manager you seek may not be the one that wins all of the popularity contests, in fact sometimes the most effective manager can be the one that does so in a quiet and integrated fashion giving attention to the organization and team versus themselves.

The manager we all seek to work for and top-notch manager that we all seek to be has certain traits that are noticeable if you look in the right places. The following delves into the traits that a professional manager strives for to be the best manager they can possibly be:

Always positive and never complaining the ideal manager presses forward every day through problems and situations. Views every situation as an opportunity to make things better and maintains an optimistic outlook toward creative and innovative solutions.

Affirmation of other's efforts through daily recognition of their work and contribution to the team; the professional manager is actively seeking efforts by other people to distinguish. They are constantly shaping behaviors through recognition of a job well done.

Delegation of decision making and responsibility to the level closest to the point of impact is something the ideal manager does to demonstrate confidence in people's ability to act responsibly and pursue improvements in the organization, for themselves and the good of the team as a whole. Authority is no good if kept close to the manager's vest. Authority is decreed from above but delegated to accomplish tasks. True managerial power comes from the floor of the organization not from the ceiling.

Meeting needs of the people within the confines of the resources available is a professional manager's ongoing task. A team member cannot be forsaken; rather a professional manager uses encouragement and guidance to back up their team members when things get tough and they are always there to advocate for them and stand beside them.

Thriftiness and monetary responsibility are a basic tenant of the ideal manager. Having a perspective that everything done must have a financial benefit to the company directly or indirectly and working to always return the investment made in people and time spent on a given task or area is a lost trait among many managers. Without the experience of owning their own business, (which I highly recommend everyone does at some point in their career), a manager can struggle to see how the tasks that their team engage in will require a pay back to the bottom-line of the company or a benefit to the recipient of the organization. The professional manager uses money to focus on the best investment of that money to drive forward significant results.

Driving for results in everything they do a professional manager keeps their eye on the end goal and measures success based on achieving results. Results achieved include tangible and intangible, financial and employee developmental goals, as well as maintaining integrity and credibility of the manager, the team, and the organization. An ideal manager knows that it is accomplishment that pays the bills, and effort rewarded by the manager, is a means to the end.

A top-notch manager is a spokesperson for the company or organization that is looked upon by others as an ambassador for the team. A professional manager makes an important statement by showing the ability to disagree with a company policy in a positive way yet when the final decision is made, to implement in a decisive and positive manner the direction given. This also means that if the company decision is immoral, illegal, unethical, or violates professionalism in managerial behavior, the model manager stands up and opposes it.

A professional manager will not succumb to an unacceptable managerial behavior. They will not compromise their professional beliefs and who they are as a professional manager for an unprofessional organization or bad decision.

A model manager understands that it is their responsibility to help develop their employees. This means identifying areas where the employees can strengthen their skills and get exposure to additional training, information, people and resources to help them grow. It also means looking out for them and opening doors to new opportunities for them to advance their careers within the company.

A model manager has turnover in his/her department through upward development of people and will attract good hard-working people who wish to advance their careers through the development and guidance that the ideal manager provides them.

Have you ever felt comfortable around a manager who is angry or shows a negative attitude or temper? Emotions have no brains in a professional manager's routine. Emotional behavior when expressed in a positive way to bolster employee excitement and enthusiasm for a task or for building department interaction is a good trait to have. However, the use of negative emotion is forbidden in the repertoire of the ideal manager.

A top-notch manager will embrace risk, calculate risk, look for areas to improve that may include risk and then demonstrate a willingness to take on risk to improve the organization. Being bold and courageous must be on the list for a manager to be successful but also the willingness to take the responsibility for the outcome of their actions. Doing what is commonplace in this world will not allow a company to differentiate themselves and can leave them in the dust amongst their competition. A true leader recognizes this and constantly strives to put their organization in the best position to succeed now and in the future.

Recognition is a staple of the ideal manager. The professional manager is always giving praise for accomplishments in a way that is effective while taking the blame when things go wrong. No one cares about the excuses, in the end it is the team that gets the job done that deserves praise and when the game is won, the professional manager leads the team on to the next game. The team moves on with a sense of determination that they will always work hard and overcome obstacles. Always looking forward to the challenges ahead of them instead of whining about what couldn't be done in the past.

Of course, the model manager understands that problems beget profits. A professional manager keeps one eye on the present and the other on the future. He/she uses failure as a springboard for improvement and continues to look ahead to the future striving constantly for excellence. The model manager maintains a balance between practical daily execution of tasks and the visionary activities that need to be developed for the future.

The best manager is the one who places a value on the human aspects of the business as well as the tactical. Time spent engaging the employees in team building activities are recognized as proper and profitable investments in the organization. Building group enthusiasm and loyalty is a trait of the professional manager.

Integrity and a track record of getting things done is a persona of the model manager and is a characteristic that proclaims what we can do and what the benefit is. He/she has the ability to execute against the implementation of the improvement to demonstrate the results that have been promised. This sets the manager apart as one that can be trusted to do what they say they are going to do. An ideal manager is a person of high integrity.

A professional manager is an ideal leader. Leadership traits abound in the familiarity that people have when they think about the person. Always appreciating the blessings and efforts of the people and their talents, giving others a sense of belonging and inspiring them to go beyond their perceived limitations both personally and professionally. A leader through action and results, a leader through the accomplishments of their department and people, and a leader who writes the book about the culture of the organization through their adherence to the discipline of doing things right for the right reasons consistent with all the traits of a professional manager.

Just as spectators see the forward score the goal in soccer and may miss all of the work the defensive midfielder did to set up the team to score, or the fans who cheer on their favorite running back in football but miss the exceptional work done by an offensive lineman to set up the game winning touchdown, such is the conspicuity of the professional manager. Finding this person will take effort as they are seldom on the front page of the news, but one thing is certain, the team is not the same if the professional manager is missing.

A True Leader

Remember that problems beget profits. Problems in the organization represent opportunities for you as a manager to demonstrate true leadership ability. A professional manager is flexible and willing to drive change to make the most out of any given situation. Demonstrating the ability to mold a situation from what would appear to most to be a desperate failure into a promising future is the trait that separates a manager from a true leader. A strong leader will adapt to the situation whether it be a person, group, or business situation. They will think through all the alternatives and make a choice to drive the team forward. They will be willing to take two steps backward to start forward again if necessary and demonstrate the wiliness and desire to change as the environment dictates. Not only do strong leaders manage stress well they thrive on managing through stressful situations showing their ability to knock barriers and obstacles out of their way. Leaders do not wait to be asked to take charge of a situation; they act impulsively and attract the acceptance of others in their efforts.

A strong leader projects the future through the vision they have for the organization. It is through the support received by the employees that professional managers drive an organization forward. All the key leadership characteristics are important to establish the respect of the workforce and gain the esteem and prestige of the people in the organization which includes peers and superiors as well. Remember nothing gets done without people seeing the need to do it. A leader provides the springboard from which the group can feel comfortable moving forward on a given path. A path that they might know they need to travel but might not otherwise pursue without the vision of the manager. A professional manager defines the path to take and communicates the benefits of going there; and then engages people in the process of determining the best method of doing it.

Moses was able to persuade the Hebrews to cross the Sea as it was parted to escape death and enslavement at the hands of the Egyptians. It takes a powerful leader with great skill and profound vision to lead people through a desolate tract like this! I wonder at the configuration of the United States of America if Abe Lincoln did not possess the characteristics of a strong and convicted leader following a vision beyond what most people in both the North and the South could see at the time. For Abe's vision and determination, we can now see the significance of the union of what is today a great, powerful, and thriving country that promotes unity and freedom for its citizens and for all peoples of the world!

A professional manager is also a great leader. The status they acquire is earned not provided or dictated. The task is challenging and difficult, but the rewards experienced through personal and professional satisfaction are tremendous. Stopping for a moment every so often to look back at accomplishments can be very fulfilling. A true leader will then turn his/her back on the accomplishments and move forward with a new vision and path to continually make things better for their people and their company or organization.

When you talk with me, I feel wanted; when there is silence, I only wonder and wait.

Chapter 11 – Successful Communications

In order to be effective as a manager, you need to achieve a successful level of communication between yourself and your employees. You also need to provide an environment that is conducive to successful communications between people and departments.

Employee Perspective

An important fact to note is that employees are reluctant to disagree. Managers often express the wish that their employees would exert more initiative; speak up and feel free to disagree. However, there are reasons why employees are frequently reluctant to speak up or disagree on various issues.

Job security is a significant factor. Employees tend to go with the flow and do not take unnecessary risks. Their personal job security is a higher priority than ruffling the manager's feathers. If the manager promotes people that agree with everything they do and say, it will be hard for an employee to risk mentioning something that is contrary. Their future employment is in the hands of their manager and they have a basic need to make sure they are on solid ground relative to the impression their manager has of their performance and contribution. Obviously, the professional manager works to encourage a variety of thoughts and ideas from their employees and rewards them for expressing their opinions when done in a constructive way.

Status barriers are real in any organization. Employees are not likely to communicate as openly and freely with a superior as they are not as comfortable in the presence of people at a higher level. A professional manager works to minimize the impact of this status difference; however, it is a real issue for employees generally.

The manager's reputation often precedes him/her and past perceptions that people have of dealing with the manager will determine how willing they are to risk disagreeing with them. In this area perception is truly reality – that does not mean that it is true. A professional manager is always sensitive to what people's perceptions are of them and work to manage relationships in a way that allow people to see them for what and who they truly are.

The previous experience in dealing with a manager predicts future experience. Everyone at some point has experienced the pain of a manager's wrath when they have disagreed or spoke up to challenge an issue. Conditioning that is born from previous experience can cause a barrier to employees' willingness to speak up in future situations. The professional manager must recognize this and work even harder to create a safe zone for employees to feel that it is okay for them to come forward without a repeat of past repercussions.

There is inherent communication strains that exist in the relationship between the workgroup and the manager that may need recognized, taken into account, and overcome if the manager is to be effective. When the manager is noticeably younger than the employees, or when the manager is new to the organization and the employees are long-term there is inherent strain. When the manager is female, and her employees are male and may be unaccustomed to a female authority figure, or the manager is a member of an ethnic minority dealing with employees in a different ethnic majority without being accustomed to a minority authority figure the result is strain. When the manager has been promoted from the workgroup that they are now responsible for managing, or the manager is less educated or trained than the employees they are responsible for there is also the potential for strain.

Employees Need Information

Employees have a desire for information about what is going on in the environment they work in. They have a need to know how decisions will affect them and communication is important for them to feel comfortable at work. Employees need information primarily for the purpose of understanding what is required of them to do their jobs. They also need information that will tell them what they want to know about the company or organization as a whole.

It is difficult for a professional manager to understand why some managers believe they can only share the information that they feel the employees can handle. It is as if the manager thinks that employees will not understand if they tell them the whole story. This leads to doubt and fear in the employees and eventually results in a lack of trust. The more open the manager is in their communication and the more readily available information is to people the more solid the manager's footing will be when walking through issues.

Employees generally relish information and will take the responsibility to seek out information as needed. As we all know communication is a two-way street. When provided information employees also have a responsibility to be receptive to what they have been given assuming the manager is forthright in the information provided.

In order to do their jobs well employees need information. They need to know what is expected of them. They need to know their job responsibilities, tasks, priorities, goals and objectives. They also need to understand the organization structure and reporting relationships. They need to know who to report issues to and how to report those issues. Employees need to know the constraints or freedoms acceptable in doing their job – what are the guardrails for them. They also need to know what the acceptable norm is for approaching a job situation or problem.

Employees need to know how the work that they do and how their workgroup fits into the overall organization. They need to know how the tasks they perform will impact the larger organization and the people that the organization interacts with and serves. It is critical that employees know how and why certain decisions are made that affect them and the company as a whole. Employees should be involved in planning and evaluation of initiatives that support decisions on things that are pertinent to their jobs and the work they do. If there are circumstances that affect their jobs and department, they need to be kept informed of all such matters.

Some of the most basic of issues can sometimes be the most important. Managers should not overlook the importance of letting employees know where and how to secure resources to do their jobs well. Where do the employees get information about how to do a job, where do they get supplies, what do they do when their computer fails to work, which number do they call when the machinery stops working, how do they get an answer to a human resource issue, etc. As you can tell this list can be extensive and contains items that a tenured employee may take for granted. The advisor or mentor program is a good way to provide a new employee support for this level of information.

An effective performance review process is a great source of information to help an employee be proficient in their job. All employees need periodic performance evaluations and feedback from their manager on strengths and development areas. This helps people know where they stand in the organization. It also provides them guidance on how to move forward in the organization. On a broader scale, not so much in the short-term, but in the long run the performance review becomes more a reflection of you as a manager than it does of the employee(s) being reviewed.

In addition to regular performance reviews against goals and objectives employees need to be informed on training resources and opportunities. All employees should receive from their manager information to guide them in their individual career and job development. Employees also need to be kept informed about their potential with the organization and be kept abreast of promotional opportunities both currently available and in the future.

The most important information a manager can provide an employee is recognition. A professional manager encourages, supports, and promotes the employees individually and as a group. The professional manager provides information in a way that demonstrates that they care about the employee as a person and not just a number. A professional manager will provide information that demonstrates fairness. They will go above and beyond to show interest in the work that each individual does and will work to keep ahead of the information flow expected by the employees. You know how good it feels when a store clerk goes beyond your expectation of service at the point of sale or when you are dealing with a quality or service problem. A professional manager provides a similar feeling when dealing with an issue facing one of their team members.

Parallel Process

In our society it is commonplace for conversations and communication to follow the path of argumentation. An argumentative approach is generally used by one person or group viewing a situation from their perspective attempting to influence or persuade another person or group to their way of thinking. Argument does have its place in certain situations, especially when both parties agree to engage in argument as a means of delving into an issue or participating in a healthy detailed review of a critical subject. At the conclusion of a healthy argument both participating individuals or groups must agree in advance to accept the outcome that provides the best benefit to the organization as a whole and then support the decision that is made as a result of the engagement.

The problem with the argumentative approach is that most people do not engage in the process for the sake of deriving a mutually beneficial outcome. Argumentation theory is an interdisciplinary study using logical reasoning to arrive at a set of conclusions across a given set of premises. Historically argumentation has been used to formulate reasons, identify and determine conclusions, validate a specific belief, and utilize results for the purpose of influencing others. The argumentative approach can be found commonly used in debate, persuasion, basic conversation and dialogue. Although a common approach used across most organizations and business situations as a professional manager you want to shift the emphasis away from an argumentative approach whenever possible. The approach that works best consists of a parallel thought process.

Parallel thinking is an effective way to get people to see multiple aspects of a given situation together instead of the traditional method of adversarial debate or argument that serves to separate. The thinking process is divided into specific parts some of which look at the situation from opposite directions. The key to the parallel process is that everyone is engaged in thinking through the issue together instead of using an adversarial approach. For both adversarial debate and parallel thinking, the objective is identified and the result to prove or disprove statements from both parties is established upfront. In the adversarial approach arguments are given by both parties along with facts to support those arguments with one party trying to outperform or win the debate over the other party.

In a parallel thinking process both parties work together to identify all the reasons why a specific position will work. Another part of the process consists of parallel discussion about what the needed resources are to support the position. Similarly, parallel thinking is used to identify additional data or facts required to explore the issue adequately. After thinking through the positive aspects of proceeding in a certain direction with an issue, the parties work together to identify all the reasons that the decision will not work. This negative mutual assessment keeps the optimistic reasoning in check and balance. The goal is to ensure that the best decision that can be made will be made. The decision must always take into consideration the practicality or true impact of the choice on the business. As you can see the parallel thought process is much better at gaining consensus and acceptance by both parties to an issue. When completed successfully everyone proceeds with no reservation concerning the direction the team is heading. The decision-making process is enhanced, and the professional manager simply follows through with the conclusions generated by the team in the engagement.

Taking a problem between two individuals or groups and making it into a profit for the team or company is a primary purpose or mission for the professional manager. In order to be successful you need to make sure you utilize all the tools available to you. Successful communication means providing the correct information in the most effective manner to engage people in a way that drives collaborative and effective performance for everyone on the team. The example you set as a manager in how you handle basic communication will set the expectation and climate for the rest of the team and will ultimately help define the culture of the organization.

Collaborate

Problem solving is basic to human survival. Decision making and problem solving are key competencies of management. Too often managers spend time trying to solve symptoms of a problem and fail to see or solve the root cause of a problem. We tend to view problem solving as a response to an emotional issue or needed to correct a failure versus a well defined and understood process that people engage in to drive improvement. We also tend to focus energy on "our" solution and ignore others in an attempt to get to resolution quickly. To improve the quality of solutions in an organization it is critical that a consistent process is developed and used. Our end goal is to recognize problems as profits and utilize an acceptable and efficient method of driving continuous improvement in the organization. By far the most effective process a professional manager can use is one that is based on a collaborative root cause problem solving approach.

What are the various levels of root cause problem identification? The first is referred to as symptoms. Symptoms are behaviors or events that demonstrate a problem exists and are representative of a failure to achieve a desired result. Causes are factors, that may be controllable or uncontrollable, that contribute to the failure. Root cause is the underlying issue or tangible object that needs addressed or changed to improve the situation and make the problem go away permanently.

Statistics show that 85% to 90% of employee motivational or attitudinal deficiencies are linked to system or process issues that fail to deal with root cause. Subsequently issues persist as problems instead of being brought to the surface and eliminated.

The most satisfying and effective method of problem solving is collaboration. Collaboration is a process that follows the path of greatest advantage versus a path of least resistance. When engaged in collaboration the parties recognize the need to solve a problem, create something better, and discover something new. It is not a common precept of our American culture to collaborate. We tend to embody a rugged individualism and a premise that people at a higher level of management in an organization produce better ideas and solutions. We tend to restrict each other in the competitive drive to live up to our position or outdo each other to prove that we are better at solving problems and identifying solutions.

Collaboration with the stakeholders of a particular issue tends to drive parallel thought processes and higher levels of employee engagement and acceptance. The combined thought processes of multiple people with varying perspectives to a problem supports the generation of solutions that are implementable and achievable. Garnering the support of everyone involved in a problem will set you up as the manager who people prefer to work with and can trust that decisions will be made taking into account all aspects of the business. People are more accepting of a solution if they believe that the manager takes to heart their concerns and opinions about the subject and will do what is right for the organization and not what will promote a select few or themselves.

In order to be effective at using collaboration and parallel problem solving and decision-making processes the professional manager removes the tension and emotion from the situation. Positive communication techniques and the ability to own a problem, team-up with others and ask for their support, listen to what others have to say, and take action to resolve the root cause of an issue will distinguish the manager that can truly lead people to change.

Communication that touches on all the basic engagement strategies works when handled in a consistent and defined manner with confidence emanating from the leader. We all know that it is much quicker to just make a decision and force the issue and sometimes people simply accept that the organization operates in this fashion. Overwhelmingly the organization that takes the time upfront to involve people in a collaborative process will in the long run come up with better results. Initially there will be apprehension and anxiety when moving from a basic problem-solving approach to a new collaborative process. The key is to manage the communication process by using a confident messaging approach that converts people to a new viewpoint. If you can present the new way of thinking to the group in a self-assured manner you can assist in releasing the tension associated with the change and do so in a positive manner.

Deliver with Confidence

The difference between confident presentations and ones that end up as complete disasters reside in the presenter's ability to channel the tension and fear associated with the process into the presentation. As a professional manager you will need to be a confident speaker and presenter. It is acceptable if you struggle to speak in front of a large group; everyone has a degree of anxiety in these situations. The best way to cope with and improve your speaking proficiency is to focus on following presentation habits that will build your confidence and success in overall communication efforts.

There are a few key points to consider in all communication exercises. You express the majority of your thoughts and attitudes nonverbally. Because of this you need to control your nonverbal expressions and be consistent in your approach. If you are passionate about the topic you are speaking about then your audience will show more interest. If you are conversely uninterested in the topic then the recipients of your message will likely be uninterested too! Practicing makes you better at what you do and in spite of your level of ability you can master an approach that will work for you. It is possible to shift feelings of anxiety into effective and impactful communication and move from inward tension to outward expressiveness.

The first step is to prepare and practice. The more you can see yourself performing well the more likely you will be to replicate the behavior on stage or in front of the audience. You should plan on rehearsing with a peer or in front of a mirror, both of these methods work. Visualize the presentation in your mind. This approach prepares you to deliver the same performance live when required.

Develop a strong belief in the topic and commit yourself to the task of making sure others share your interest and passion in the subject. Building and reinforcing relationships prior to the session will help with managing the potential for disagreement and will support your confidence under pressure if you know that you have allies in the audience. You should contact key stakeholders in advance and ask them for ideas, help, and support for the topic so that you can rely on them for support if needed during the presentation.

The objective is to communicate effectively not perform or put on a show to entertain people. Pretend like you are engaged in a conversation with a couple of people you trust and make eye contact with those people as you are speaking. In essence you are simply conversing with a large group of people in the same way you would with a few people you know well. Using this approach helps with tension management.

Relax and channel tension in your body before and during the presentation. Work the tension from the part of the body where you notice it the most or start from the neck and shoulders down to your feet taking deep breaths and relaxing muscles. Stretch and tighten a muscle group and then release and relax that group as you remove the stress. Control your breathing. Take deep breaths before starting and then get your breathing into a relaxing and rhythmic pattern.

If you make a mistake either acknowledge it openly or pick up where you stumbled and move on taking control and command over the situation. People will likely forget that you stumbled if you do not let it affect your presentation.

Relax and be satisfied in your preparation and tell yourself that you have the knowledge and qualifications required to speak on the topic to the group. Do not tighten up in your preparation to the point that you cannot adjust and be flexible where needed in the presentation process. The more you interact and engage in the conversation with your audience the more likely you are to forget about your tension and feelings and focus on the feelings of the people you are speaking to. Above all be positive; if you believe you can do it then most likely you will do well.

Communication Strategy

A survey of top companies suggests that formal communications within a company meet certain criteria when noted as successful. The CEO sets the example demonstrating the importance of employee communication. All employee communication is tied to specific company or business unit strategies. Many companies have a corporate communication department that is included in the initial process when designing and implementing changes within the company and business units. The most common structure is a centralized communication department for strategic planning with execution performed by business unit leadership and management. Toolkits are developed for choosing the correct methods to use for any strategic project. Companies that are successful in their communication programs have a common trait; communication is most effectively used to positively reinforce employee behaviors that demonstrate company mission and objectives.

In these top companies all management levels are held accountable for effective employee communication. Communication responsibility is included in the manager's performance review. The human resource department provides training and mandatory certification in employee communications. The manager's toolbox includes significant emphasis on face-to-face communication.

To make sure that communication plans and messages meet the intended objective internal advisory boards and employee surveys are used. Annual employee surveys are performed to measure employee communication effectiveness by business unit. Internal communication advisory boards are used to provide feedback and make recommendations on methods to use for specific business objectives. This is another effective way to engage employees in the overall communication process and in the business in general.

Most executives agree that employee communication is essential to the success of the organization. There is definitely a link between effective employee communication and employee engagement. Engagement happens when employees know how they fit into the company strategy.

An underlying assumption in most communication programs is that management is not communicating enough, and that communication is not getting to all employees. In an effective program there must be a consistent method of measuring the impact of communication efforts. The program needs to consist of a way to incorporate feedback from employees. Among managers there needs to be an effective level of information sharing so that messages and feedback flows throughout all levels of the organization. The amount of communication, the methods used, the consistency of the messages, and the timing of the communication is essential.

A key point to consider in your communication process is for you to know what employees need to know. What are the benefits of the communication being provided and how do we measure it? How do you get feedback from employees? How do you respond to employee feedback? Areas to consider include knowing what information is necessary for employees to do well in their day to day jobs, ability to assess the value of the recommendations being made to improve the process, identifying where a lack of communication is creating performance issues, and what tools are necessary to support the program.

Solutions to the communication process involve ways to better define and measure the current level of success in the program. You want to always train and reward the behavior that supports the objective you are trying to achieve. Communication and recognition must flow from top down and bottom up within the organization with no breakdown in the middle. To avoid the gap, you must talk about what you want and expect from all levels of management to support the communication process.

Message content and message delivery is very important. To be effective you need to tell people what they want to know from their point of view. Always let people know what's in it for them. Communicate in a manner that speaks to the average employee. Your message should be so clear that the newest employee understands it. Messages need to be clearly defined and tied to specific goals. People need to know what we are working on and what our business unit strategy is to get there. Communication should focus on the positives and successes within the business unit.

Some believe that you should only communicate what employees need to know. As long as the messages are linked to the business unit and relevant to employee understanding of the objective it is best to share as much information as possible with them. Remember everyone has different needs – one size does not fit all. Some messages will need adjusted to fit a specific audience. In all cases explain the "Why's" of the goals and objectives. Above all let employees know why they are important. Employees enjoy recognition and information regarding their department. Employees want to be appropriately thanked for their hard work and effort.

When putting together your communication plan a professional manager will maintain a healthy balance. Keep the number of meetings to a minimum and adopt a belief in using multiple methods to communicate. Give a sense of belonging to the team. Make sure that what you communicate is perceived as valuable and pertinent. Provide options to employees and ask for ideas on how to structure the process. Be concise and factual, specific and actionable, candid and non-political. Remember a professional manager takes the initiative recognizing that communication is driven top down in each business unit. Your efforts will either succeed or fail based on your level of commitment to the process and the emphasis you place on employee communication.

The trail we have traveled becomes our path every day;
seeking truth from the present gives us strength in our way.

Chapter 12 – Build a Supportive Culture

The professional manager creates a culture of mutual cooperation and trust. A professional manager shows passion for doing things. When generated by the manager to a level where the energy is reverberating off the walls people get excited about their involvement. People in a supportive climate feel good about being a part of the team. Building an emphasis on the team nature of the work being done is very important in building a supportive climate. A supportive climate is not one where the manager drives change and the employees obey. A team spirit requires all players to be engaged to win the game. The coach that gets players excited about doing well can go only so far if all the players do not mutually respect and reciprocate by showing the same passion and emotion in doing the best they can to win the game.

A professional manager serves the people that he/she represents and is not to be viewed as a judge. When a receiver takes his eye off the ball and drops the pass, the last thing he needs is a coach who judges him when he walks to the sideline. A professional receiver knows what he did wrong, what the player needs is a coach that will provide encouragement and support for the athlete and a willingness to put them back on the field with a chance to do better.

A receiver who is handled in the above-mentioned fashion will work harder to catch the next pass and will do so not only so they look good, but to make the team and the coach look good as well. It is based on cooperation and mutual trust that the team gets better. The receiver must look for and communicate ideas and suggestions for them to improve or for the team to execute better on the next play. What action is the employee going to commit to? What are they committing to do to improve the situation? The employee must provide feedback, come forward with process improvement ideas, think through work effort improvements, and show a sense of concern to make the environment a supportive one versus a one-way street from manager to employee. The professional manager encourages and reinforces this employee behavior.

All goals and objectives for the team must be realistic and agreed on as fair and reasonable. There must be a minimum acceptable standard for the work being done that is also viewed as fair by the team. The manager must provide the resources and training, systems and process support to enable the team to execute against the objectives they are given. The manager must prioritize, delegate, remove obstacles, include people in the decision-making process, hold people accountable, evaluate performance and provide recognition in a fair and equitable manner. A supportive climate exists when the manager and employees agree upon the reasonableness of the objectives they are held accountable to and the fairness in which the boss manages the team toward the achievement of the objectives.

Positive Communications

When the manager shows that he/she cares for the employees as individuals, demonstrates genuine listening skills and a desire to hear and receive feedback in a manner that creates an open and non-threatening environment positive communication can be achieved. The key is the relationship between the manager and the employee. A professional manager will build a strong relationship through support, accessibility, and open communication processes.

A professional manager does not put stock into titles when assembling his/her team; they work diligently to promote team support. A feeling of mutual support is critical to a positive communication environment. The manager communicates what is important by his/her words and actions. I once had a boss who spent zero time talking with me about what I felt was important in the department and did not include me or confide in me regarding the business. Instead the manager made a point out of meeting protocol. The team was berated for not arriving to the weekly staff meeting early, one of the attendees who could not make it was degraded in front of their peers, another was degraded behind their back, another was told in a demeaning tone to stop making notes on their laptop, and another was humiliated for checking their phone. Throughout the entire meeting it seemed like all the presentations were made for the manager's benefit. People were cautious about what they volunteered and said; they tightened up and moved through their material superficially trying to avoid being questioned by the manager. No open discussion occurred between people and the meeting became a weekly drudgery.

At the end of the first meeting the employees' focus was on determining what to say and what not to say, how the administrative assistant could reserve the room early and get everything setup, so we could start early without fail. The team even discussed behind the manager's back how they would explain to a customer that they had to leave a meeting early even if they were engaged in resolving a problem for them so they could get to the managers weekly meeting early. What if they were late for the meeting because of an urgent issue or problem; how would they be able to explain the reason to the manager before the meeting started especially if they are tied up on the phone with a customer? What the manager asked for he got in this situation, his people were always on time and attended the weekly meeting. The team members did not fully engage and department communication with the boss continued to be a struggle. The boss created an environment where turn-over continued among the team. For the most part only the people who could not find employment elsewhere remained with the company. The emphasis that the manager places on certain segments of the business and the behaviors he/she attempts to control determines the focus and success of the team.

As a professional manager you find ways to engage people in your communication efforts; not punish them with the communication vehicle. The manager who encourages hard work, a sense of obligation and respect for people's ability to prioritize and get meaningful work done in a responsible way will never have a problem with the team making the meeting on time. Why; because the employees want to attend the weekly meeting where they can exchange ideas and thoughts about the business with each other and their manager. They want to attend a meeting where they will get recognition for their thoughts and experience, not just for their attendance. Positive communication is not created from authority, control, and flexing managerial ego and power. In the team approach all participants can be equals and contribute without fear or apprehension. Employee tenure, position, title, etc. are minimized in the team setting. Every player is a valuable player in this endeavor.

Team members need to be open and accessible to each other in addition to openness from the manager to the team. All are equal in this regard and share in the responsibility to communicate openly with each other. The key to open communication is the feeling that a person can express their thoughts and ideas without fear of criticism or retaliation. Open communication also minimizes gossip and rumors as team members feel that they are informed and have the information they need to focus on their tasks and objectives.

Positive communication is achieved when everyone feels they have been able to share their thoughts and ideas, that they have been listened to and taken seriously and respectfully, and that they are welcomed into the group as a valued and needed member. All team members feel that they are important and belong when they are working for a professional manager.

Employee Engagement

The best ideas you will ever implement will come primarily from the workforce. Employees at floor level know the business at the point of impact where costs are incurred, service and quality are defined, and the culture of the company is displayed. Engaging employees who do the work in the decision-making process can be a scary thing for most managers. As you develop an employee engagement experience you will find that in order to gain control, you must give up control. In order to receive responsible behavior from your employees you need to treat them as responsible contributors to the organization. In order to gain respect as a manager from your employees, you must treat them with respect.

There are many ways to engage employees in the business. Involving them in cross-functional and technical groups with a specific purpose are effective means of engagement. Participation and engagement teams can take on multiple forms within an organization. Some examples are:

- Diversity committee
- Communication committee
- Training and development committee
- Project task forces
- Operational Efficiency committee
- Safety committee
- Emergency response teams
- Employee event planning committee
- Cultural improvement team
- Sanitation/quality management teams
- Customer service improvement task force

People love to be heard and to know that their ideas have been considered and even applied to the organization with positive results. This success will breed an ongoing flow of fresh and innovative suggestions and energy among the workforce. It also provides a level of acceptance for the changes made; the impact of the changes to the people and their jobs to support the improvements will be viewed in a positive light. Automatic recognition and job enrichment for your people are at your fingertips as a manager if you engage your people in the department management process utilizing employee engagement strategies.

Let's take another look at employee engagement from the perspective of the employee. Actually, let's take the subject down to the most fundamental level of the human condition and see how the actions of one person toward another affect us. When a person is under anguish and stress brain scans show high levels of pressure and restriction of blood flow – we will refer to the scan as showing a lot of red in the brain. When a person relaxes the red starts to diminish and blood flow and ability to function improves. It is interesting that the same scans show an enhanced condition – we will refer to as blue – when a person is smiling and having fun. When a person laughs the brain fills with blue in the scans and the functions in the brain exceed an average level. Clearly a person who feels comfortable and joyous in the activities they are engaged in achieves performance at a much higher level.

Research also relates that the condition stems from a natural reaction to a sense of being and belonging. It is most prevalent when a person has someone who cares for them and loves them. A spiritually fulfilling sense and a feeling of love also exist in these situations when a human can relate to who they are and are comfortable in their present condition. A welcoming environment and a sense of belonging exist for us when we feel these sensations. It can motivate us to step a little higher and walk with more confidence in the things that we do because we feel the support from those who we live and work with. A welcoming and accepting environment can be provided by a manager as easily as a parent can welcome a child, or a good Samaritan can by helping another in need. The key actions that enable this welcoming condition are captured below from the recipients' perspective. People claim to feel a sense of belonging and feel welcome when others:

- ➢ Look them in the eye
- ➢ Smile in a caring manner at them
- ➢ Use their first name
- ➢ Talk with them without seeming hurried

- Pay attention and notice when they are gone and show recognition and welcome when they return
- Ask them to participate with them in something that they can help with
- Give them a chance to help without restricting them
- Involve and include them in an activity or group
- Look to them for their advice and their opinion and show that they care, and they have listened by incorporating their suggestion somehow
- Show recognition and appreciation for their participation and contribution

Employing these behaviors into your everyday interactions with people will not only set you apart as a leader but will help you build lasting and meaningful relationships with people both inside and outside of the workplace.

Eliminate Barriers

Whatever you do, if an employee asks you for a pencil, get them a pencil! I learned this lesson as a young supervisor. No matter how many things need to get done immediately and no matter how important those things seem to the operation at the time, if an employee needs a pencil to do their job and they ask you for one, not only should you get him/her the pencil, you should do it with a degree of importance and sense of urgency. When you do that the employee knows that you feel that their needs and their contribution are just as important as anyone else in the organization. If you work hard to get your employees what they need and eliminate the things that block them from doing a good job, they will respect you as a manager and perform. In some cases, the barriers are psychological in nature and if viewed too pragmatically, a manager may dismiss the employee concern and ignore the issue. Taking time to listen to an employee who is dealing with a real or perceived restriction to their ability to perform gives you an opportunity to explore and discuss the situation and work proactively with the employee to get around, over, or through the barrier, or eliminate it entirely. It is the simple things that count the most. How you respond to employee concerns makes a huge difference in how you are viewed as a manager by your employees.

Management Focus

Today you hear about many different approaches to management and how the focus you choose as a manager can make you better. From the one-minute manager, to the customer focused manager, to data driven management, leadership focused management, managing big, managing small, change management, micromanagement, process management, etc. What has become clear to me as a manager and what has provided the greatest success and satisfaction is an employee-centered focus of management.

Too many people focus on the wrong things in business. Many managers lose sight of the importance of the one thing that will provide the greatest success to them as a manager . . . the people who do the work. Compare the focus of a manager who spends the majority of his/her energy on the needs of their boss and senior management. A boss-centered focus of management may appear on the surface to be the right approach, after all everyone needs to listen to their boss and do the tasks assigned to them. But when the manager's focus becomes centered on what the boss thinks and wants versus what the employees think and want a separation occurs that can be detrimental to the manager.

An employee-centered focus provides a manager the ability to refute and enhance ideas and directives to the betterment of the operation as a whole when taking into account the needs of the people who do the work, what the business is capable of doing, and the desires of senior management for the organization. A manager must be responsive to his/her employees, his/her bosses, and to internal and external customers all at the same time. It is a balancing act that requires the correct knowledge, experience and communication networks to be effective. Grounding your management sensitivity to the point of impact, where the work gets done, to an employee-centered focus will give you the insight to drive improvements in the operation without senior management needing to make the request.

As a manager you should always set your sights on overachieving plans and budgets, innovating and improving the operation before the need for change is required, and doing so with the support of your people who follow your lead in overachieving in everything they do. Why is this important? Who doesn't want to work for a manager who recognizes and rewards overachievement of goals and manages people based on the results and contributions they make versus a manager who promotes only those who say what the boss wants to hear or does only what the boss directs them to do.

A truly results-oriented style of management is found closely linked to an employee-centered focus of management where a business is demonstrating true growth and change on an on-going basis and has accepted change and over-achievement as the norm in their organizational culture.

The customer may not always be right, but the customer is always the customer.

Chapter 13 – Meet Customer's Needs

For every employee in every organization there is a customer. Many people have jobs where they do not interact directly with the end customer, but what they do or don't do could have a real influence on the customer's service experience. Internal customers are just as important as external customers. Adopting the mentality as a manager that your department is in the business of serving customers whether they are internal or external or a combination of both can be an effective way of creating a productive workgroup.

Using the guidelines that all businesses use to evaluate the importance of customer service in the market will help you as a manager as you communicate and adopt these same principals to the work that your team does. Remember, these guidelines apply to internal customers as well as external.

Emphasize Service and Differentiate

Just satisfying customers no longer works in today's world because:
> ➢ Customers are more demanding
> ➢ Customers are better informed, and information is at their fingertips
> ➢ Companies have more competition because customers have more choices

Progressive businesses define service as:

- ➢ Going beyond expectations and creating positive stories
- ➢ Emphasizing the people behind the product or service they provide
- ➢ Adding value to the products or services they provide
- ➢ Differentiate themselves through the lens of customer experiences

There are a few basic requirements for you and your team:
- ➢ Make sure as a manager you hire the right person for the right job
- ➢ Provide on-going customer service training
- ➢ Use salesmanship in interactions with internal and external customers
- ➢ As a manager you must also be a salesperson with employees, peers, and senior executives

Focus on All-Out Recovery

It is a shame in today's world that whenever you receive good service, it is an exception and you are excited about it! Find ways to keep the message vivid to your team that good service should be the minimum and that great service is what we want to provide all the time.

Resolving a complaint is the fastest way to create an outstanding service reputation. Generally expectations are that nothing will happen. Therefore, people usually do not complain. A problem is a golden opportunity to go beyond expectations and create a story.

Traditional businesses see complaints as an interruption. In order to deal with problems they develop a complaint department. When management gets involved in a customer service problem the traditional business response is a short-term knee-jerk reaction.

Here are five steps to a progressive recovery strategy:

1. Actively look for complaints
2. Push responsibility as close as possible to the point of impact, the place where the work gets done
3. Analyze the situation and ask "what if" questions
4. Make it easy for customers to provide feedback and be open to incoming complaints
5. Track, measure, and correct (problems, mistakes, complaints, etc.)

Turn Dissatisfaction into Loyalty

Use salesmanship when things are going wrong and you need to reconcile differences or simply repair damage that has occurred due to the actions or lack of performance by you or your team. Start by taking care of your internal customer person-to-person and be sensitive to their feelings.

When your customer is dissatisfied, forget the usual idea of a profit. Scrap whatever you thought was originally there for benefit and realize that to gain you may have to start over. Don't panic; problems do not signal the end, merely the beginning. Remember problems beget profits when approached properly and constructively.

Listen actively and let customers blow off steam. Focus on customer's feelings and make sure that you accurately paraphrase in your own words what the customer has told you. Always keep the 3 C's: Cool, Calm, and Collected.

Tell the unsatisfied customer that you are sorry. Ask what they want to make up for the damage caused by the problem that has occurred. After you have dealt with the person and their feelings, solve the problem. Act with a sense of urgency and concern for making sure things get done right. Complete the process by making a peace offering.

A White House study from the Office of Consumer Affairs provides statistics that can guide you as a manager to understand how people react to the service that your team provides them:

> - 96% of unhappy customers never complain
> - 90% of unsatisfied customers will not buy again or come back to you for service
> - Each of those unhappy customers will tell their story to at least nine other people (face-to-face; with internet and social media this could be significantly higher)
> - 13% will tell their story to more than 20 people

Although the study was performed to assist businesses with their customers, the key points related to the reaction of customers to the service they receive can be applied to internal customers that your team supports.

There are five reasons customers switch:

1. 3% leave or move away
2. 5% develop other relationships
3. 9% feel that the price/cost is too high

4. 14% are dissatisfied with the product quality or results of what was provided
5. 68% because of the way they were treated

Positioning yourself to respond to a customer post problem is important. After a problem has occurred or you have received a complaint it is imperative to maintain your internal customer support network. Using some of the wording below and hitting all the key resolution points can help you as a manager maintain credibility:

"I am sorry for the inconvenience you experienced . . . Unfortunately, sometimes there are errors made; however, it is our desire to catch and correct all problems before we serve our customers. I want to thank you for taking the time to bring your problems to our attention. It is the feedback we get from our customers that helps us to serve all of our clientele better. We take every complaint into deep consideration. It is customers, like yourself, who help make us better because you speak up to say that you care and let us know of any problems affecting you. I will personally dig into the issue and get back to you immediately with a resolution for the problem. If there is anything else we can do to make our service better, please let me know."

Remember: the customer may not always be right, but the customer is always the customer.

You cannot move a mountain, but you can climb to the top and enjoy the view.

Chapter 14 – Evaluate and Develop Team

As a young supervisor in the warehouse I learned a lot about setting goals and achieving goals. My first job in distribution was spent tracking employee performance across multiple departments and job functions. Back then we tracked all the individual and group performance metrics by hand using pencil and paper. The automated part of our job was an adding machine with rolled paper! Everyone knew what the goal was for each job function and everyone received feedback every day on their individual performance and the team performance.

Once a year all the supervisors put together a plan for their departments to identify key areas of improvement. We all had certain production goals that we had to achieve that were given to us by the operations management team. In addition to the goals provided to us we came up with two or three goals that each of us created to drive additional improvements in our departments. We prepared the tracking reports, established the baseline, and set the goal-line to hit. We then presented our goals and plans to senior management in an MBO (Management by Objectives) session. We also shared the goals with our teams in an initial launch, then followed-up with our teams reviewing progress in accordance with the communication plan that we developed to support our project.

At a young age I was able to learn the basics of goal setting and performance management which was a valuable experience for me. The fundamental basics I learned during this time I have repeated and leaned on throughout my career as a manager. The simplicity of the process, the ownership of the goal and the metric, the understanding of what needs to change in the business to achieve the objective, the importance of communication along with engagement of the team, and the persistence and determination to drive forward to hit and exceed a goal all culminated in the basics of team evaluation and development for me. These basics are the pillars of performance management that I use today.

Performance Planning

Establishing Plans and Goals

As a manager you will need to know how to establish effective plans and develop effective performance and goal measurement mechanisms. It is also important to know how to set up processes that carry out those plans. Effective leaders begin the planning process with the organization's vision and goals and end up with specific plans to achieve those goals. Plans and goals will generally involve other people, other departments, the management of potential risks and the drive to move the organization forward. It is important that the manager's and department's work schedule and resource capacity supports the entire planning process and is capable of setting and achieving the desired goals.

Here are some points and key tips to consider when establishing plans and goals:

Make sure you have allowed enough time to make the goal date achievable taking into account the routine business needs that you and your team will face throughout the goal period (year). Communicate changes to members of the team and to those affected. Are your department or team goals consistent with the organization's direction and strategic goals? Always involve those affected by a plan or goal in the creation of it. Make sure your employees are involved in setting goals and making the connection to align their goals with the team or organization's strategic plan. Employees should provide input on specific objectives, priorities and timetables. Ask your employees how their goals contribute to the organization's success. If they can't tell you, help them translate strategic goals into specific objectives.

Identify the critical path to achieve your goals. Identify assumptions underlying your direction or planning efforts that if wrong, will cause major problems. Use plans to guide your work but recognize that changes and the unexpected will occur. Once you develop your plan, ask others to identify potential problems and use their feedback to help adjust goals or come up with contingency plans. Anticipate and develop strategies to deal with critical constraints to executing the plan.

Review resource allocation to determine whether you are allocating according to your priorities and whether it is consistent with the goals that you have set. For larger projects or goals, break into several steps with specific goals and deadlines and track completion of each step to assure success of the overall plan. Set aside time every day or week to review plans and goals, and update activities. If goal dates are missed, find out why and incorporate your learning into the next planning process. Take action to address any shortcomings with the goals that have been set. Monitor and review the plan regularly to evaluate ways to improve the process in the future.

Performance Reviews

Your engagement and emphasis on the performance review process is critical to establishing guidelines and boundaries that employees need to feel secure in the employee/manager relationship. When you approach the process in the proper manner and set the tone that you are an instrument to support employee recognition and growth and not a threat to their work experience you will succeed as a manager. For those employees who are attempting to get by doing as little as possible, you will set the expectations and provide the disciplines necessary to make the workplace fair for everyone and establish the expectations of performance for the individual and the team. Use effective performance planning and goal setting processes to build your manager credibility and respect. There are ten key elements to keep in mind as a manager with the employee performance review process:

1. Without a plan in place the organization may suffer from a lack of direction
2. People need to know what is expected of them; goals need to be S.M.A.R.T.
3. People need to know that their manager acknowledges that they are doing their job
4. The performance evaluation and goal planning process provide needed structure in the workplace
5. Too few or too many goals can be a problem; ideally an employee should have three to five goals to work on over the course of a year

6. The performance evaluation should consist of evaluations for specific goals as well as an evaluation of the employee's performance against key competencies relevant to the position
7. Giving an employee an exceptional rating without the examples and facts to support the higher performance rating does not create a growth-oriented work environment
8. In addition, using examples of behavior aligned with an employee goal and competency provides a framework for a manager to improve and correct undesirable behavior or recognize good behavior while documenting the justification for the rating applied
9. The performance review should never be a surprise to an employee; frequent discussions should occur between the employee and the manager throughout the review period as needed for improvement as well as recognition
10. In the end; the performance rating a manager gives to his/her employee(s) is more a reflection of the manager's performance than it is of the employee(s) receiving the evaluation

SMART Goals

Goals need to be S.M.A.R.T. (Specific, Measurable, Attainable, Relevant, and Time-bound).

Specific

The goal is clear and unambiguous; without vagaries and platitudes. To make goals specific, they must tell a team exactly what's expected; why it's important, who's involved, where it's going to happen, and which attributes are important.

A specific goal will usually answer the five 'W' questions:

1. What: What do I want to accomplish?
2. Why: Specific reasons, purpose or benefits of accomplishing the goal
3. Who: Who is involved?
4. Where: Identify a location
5. Which: Identify requirements and constraints

Measurable

If a goal is not measurable it is not possible to know whether a team is making progress toward successful completion. Measuring progress is supposed to help a team stay on track, reach its target dates and experience the exhilaration of achievement that spurs it on to continued effort required to reach the ultimate goal.

A measurable goal will usually answer questions such as:

*   How much?
*   How many?
*   How will I know when it is accomplished?
*   Indicators should be quantifiable

Attainable

Goals must be realistic and also attainable. An attainable goal will stretch a team in order to achieve it without the goal being extreme. Goals should not be out of reach or below standard performance otherwise they become meaningless. An attainable goal should allow goal-setters to identify previously overlooked opportunities to bring themselves closer to the achievement of their goals.

An achievable goal will usually answer the question how:

- How can the goal be accomplished?
- How realistic is the goal based on other constraints?

Relevant

You will need support to accomplish a goal: resources, sponsors, etc. and therefore a solid business reason to focus time and energy in a given area. Goals that are relevant to the hierarchy of goals from your boss and the management team, when cascaded down through the organization, as well as goals that are important to your team, will receive that needed support.

Relevant goals (when met) drive the team, department and organization forward. A goal that supports or is in alignment with other goals is considered a relevant goal. A relevant goal can answer yes to these questions:

- Does this seem worthwhile?
- Is this the right time?
- Does this match our other efforts/needs?
- Are you the right person?
- Is it applicable in the current socio-economic environment?

Time-bound

Goals must be grounded within a timeframe by means of a set target date. A commitment to a deadline helps a team focus their efforts on completion of the goal on or before the due date. This is intended to prevent goals from being overtaken by the day-to-day crises that invariably arise in an organization. A time-bound goal is intended to establish a proper sense of urgency.

A time-bound goal will usually answer the question:

- When?
- What can I do six months from now?
- What can I do six weeks from now?
- What can I do today?

Development Planning

There are ten fundamental considerations to take into account when approaching the employee development process. It is helpful to review the areas from a personal perspective and then apply what is relative to the employee that you are coaching or mentoring:

Get Specific

What interpersonal skill needs addressed? To find out more about what your need is go ask a few people who you trust to tell you what they see. In order to do this, you need to first accept that you have a need. Everyone has skills that can improve so there is no shame in asking for help from others who care.

It is good to get specific examples of when, where, with who, in what settings, under what conditions, and how many times the examples have occurred. Do they know of anyone that can help you? Take notes of the examples and thank them for their feedback.

Create the Plan

Your plan is simple; write down the things that you should stop doing, the things you need to start doing, and the things you need to keep doing. Use the examples from the step above to assist in this process and once identified, ask others for help with this need.

Learn from Others

Observe and model the behavior of others who demonstrate strength in the skill that you desire to improve. Look for just one trait in a person and for multiple traits that you wish to model; identify multiple people, each who is strong at that particular trait. Sort through the behaviors as you model and keep the good, throw away the bad.

Get a Partner

It helps to have a partner to bounce ideas and situations against. Find someone who is working on the same or similar skills and share experiences on what has worked and what hasn't to support your activities and provide helpful reassurance as needed.

Get Periodic Feedback

Split your time between two different groups of people, those who know you well and may have helped with your initial skill identification, and those who are new and do not know you as well. See if the feedback you receive from both groups correlate with each other. Recognize that the newer people will see improvement quicker as they do not have a lagging perception with having no previous basis to compare with what you have or haven't done in the past.

Learn from a Course

Take a course where you can learn from the material and practice the competency or skill. Apply undivided focus to the material and take notes that are relevant to your situation. Use this as a reference source of material to build on in practical application which can be used to gain a deeper understanding of the impact and basis of the skill you are developing.

Do Research

Surf through the world of business books and scan the outline of content provided until you find one or two that speak to the areas you are interested in improving. Your initial study may lead you to read additional books and subjects that support your work.

Learn from Famous People

Learn from real people and how they developed the skills that they are known for. Autobiographies can be a good source for modeling behavior and establishing a target to shoot for or person to emulate.

Apply Stretching Tasks

Seventy percent of all skill development happens on-the-job. Start small by identifying tasks that you need to engage in to stretch out of your current comfort zone and into the areas you have identified for development focus. Skill development can also occur through community involvement as well and may be a means to get started in an area of skill improvement that can then carry over to the workplace.

Track Progress

What gets measured gets done. This is especially true for something that is important to your personal and professional development as there may be tasks that you complete that are initially only apparent to you. That is okay. You need to measure your progress and apply intrinsic reward for your accomplishments so that you stay on the path you have established for yourself.

Individual Development Action Planning Guide

The following format can be used to assist in the initial individual development action planning process. As a manager you may use this approach to pull out the need for improvement in a given area for one of your employees. This helps you to bring attention to an area where you believe there is a need for a specific skill improvement.

You can also use this format to provide a platform for an individual (including yourself) to identify skill development needs and the action steps for improvement.

As an individual development planning guide this is designed to help make the person using it better in the areas that they see a need or have a desire to improve.

Here is an outline of the development template to get you started:

1) Key Focus Area
   - What do I want to change or develop?
   - What areas of focus provide the most benefit in my career plan?

2) Daily Action Plan
   - What helps me signal to put a new development behavior into action?
   - What new behavior will I try and where will I push my comfort zone?
   - Every time I see the following situation(s) . . . I will take the following development action(s): (List up to five)

3) Reflection Focus
   - What will I do to help reflect on my development progress, what worked, what didn't work, and what do I want to do next time?

4) Feedback and Support
   - What is my plan to seek feedback from others, track my progress, gather advice, and progress with my learning?

5) Transfer Learning to the Next Level
   - How frequently will I review progress?

- When will I update my development plan?
- How will I use what I have learned to aid in my development?

Development Opportunities Matrix

There are numerous reference materials and books available on competencies and skill development that can guide you in identifying the exact behavior to improve and suggestions on how to do it. The opportunity matrix is a short list that is intended to provide ideas on what to include in the development plan.

Project and Special Assignments
- Broad or stretch goals
- Rotate between areas
- Temporary or on-going

Cross-Functional Moves
- Exposure to Change
- New Dept and Functions
- Shift between Line vs Staff
- Spend time with other teams

Project Teams and Committees
- Brainstorm new ideas
- Discuss new programs & current issues
- Participate in one-time event
- Experience with presentations

Development and Startups
- Work with a new team
- Participate in new systems/processes

Look for On-the-job Opportunities
- Signup for new projects or assignments
- Replace people on vacation
- Volunteer for temporary assignments
- Assume lead responsibilities for team
- Process/procedure enhancement

Develop in Current Position
- Use Mentor programs
- Take on more responsibility
- Assignment of individual projects
- Work on perspective building tasks
- Take on a difficult task or challenge

Identify Off-the-Job Opportunities
- Participate in community groups
- Experiment on new tasks as a volunteer
- Give presentations to groups

Education and Formal Training/Development
- Professional certifications
- Technical training courses
- Leadership skill development
- Executive forums and shadowing

Self-Development
- Reading and self-study
- Professional organizations
- College/University programs
- Seminars

Individual Development Goals

It is always good to pick two or three short term objectives that focus on the current job. Short term can be defined as no more than twelve months. Choose one or two long-term objectives that will help prepare for the next step on a possible career ladder. Consider the next one to two years as the long-term developmental window. Enter the goals in an individual development goal tracking sheet and as you would for performance goals, make sure that the development goals are also S.M.A.R.T. (Specific, Measurable, Attainable, Relevant, and Time-bound).

Individual Development Goal Tracking Sheet

The goal tracking sheet should be simple and easy to use and understand. It should be comprised of four sections that describe the goals and action plans for both short and long-term objectives. In the objective section describe the goal in terms of the competency or skill that is the main area of focus.

The first section of the development tracking sheet needs to include objectives. Short-term objectives should include what to learn more about to do the current job more effective over the next twelve months. Long-term objectives include what to learn more about to be a better candidate for a future position with a focus over the next one to two years. The tracking sheet needs to include action steps, resources, time period, and measurement components. Lastly the tracking must include completion dates for all activities and room for notes and comments.

I learned a valuable management lesson years ago listening to one of Father Bob's homilies. He told us that closest to our greatest strengths are our greatest weaknesses. I reflected on that message and started to see it come to life for me, right in front of my eyes, in my daily routine. Every area that I felt strong and well developed was an area I was able to see that in some situations that trait made me weak and vulnerable. For instance, working long hours and working hard taking very few breaks and driving tough for results was definitely a strength that I was proud of. At the same time this drive for results and the hard work that I performed could at times alienate me from others and from my family. It created a lack of balance in my work and home life.

Do not be surprised as you put together a development plan for yourself or one of your employees that you see patterns that speak to a strength that is also an area for further development. Many successful development plans work on expanding existing strengths and focus on competency balance. Guiding a person to accentuating existing visible or hidden strengths is a satisfying and meaningful purpose of managing people.

As a professional manager, it is your responsibility to develop your team and your people. Being an instrument for your employee's career success will provide a steady stream of talented and aspiring individuals that want the opportunity to work on your team and benefit from the development you provide them. Losing good people to promotions within the company is the goal and is not a threat to the manager who develops his/her team members.

A professional athlete is one who gets paid for what he/she does; a professional manager gets paid with respect from the people they work with every day.

Chapter 15 – You are a Professional Manager

This book has provided guidance on basic fundamental management skills that are critical to your success as a manager. However it is just a small portion of all of the areas that you as a manager are responsible to your organization. There are many volumes on management of business and people today and there are many great seminars, books, courses, internet materials and studies that you can learn from in your career as a manager. The most important school you can attend as a manager is the work setting. The best teachers you will find are your employees. And, when you have the opportunity to work with a great leader or manager as a peer or your boss or even one of your employees; take the opportunity to learn from your relationships and improve your skill as a manager.

No two people manage alike. A wide variety of people with various personality types can be great leaders. Great leaders and great managers are not stamped out of a mold. Many are groomed from within with help from someone who saw potential in them. There is very likely potential in you that you might not have even realized yet! Surround yourself with good people who are good leaders and managers. Let them help you pull the potential from inside you and aspire to always be better at what you do. Take on your position as a manager as a profession and in spite of what happens in the work world around you, be the best manager you can possibly be.

A professional athlete is always working out to keep muscles strong and conditioned. They are always practicing techniques and looking for ways to get better and stay sharp and competitive on the field. Think of yourself as a wide receiver. A wide-receiver is always working hard to be the best wide-receiver in the football league to keep his position on the team. Whether or not he plays for the current team or gets traded to another team he is first and foremost a professional wide receiver. His legacy will be based on what he does statistically in the position of wide-receiver, not for the win-loss records of the teams he played for.

The same is true for you as a manager. You must constantly hone your managerial skills and work to be the best manager possible regardless of what company you work for. First and foremost, you are a professional manager. To stay sharp and competitive and to continue to amass positive managerial statistics you must stick to the basics, keep working the same muscles to keep them in shape, and never assume that you know everything about managing people. A professional manager always practices basic techniques to maintain the edge needed to excel at managerial ability.

In summary, the author has attempted to provide a chronological resource of techniques to assist you in maintaining your managerial edge. The basis of these techniques has been formed over years of struggle, effort, and success in the world of managing people; based on confrontation of numerous problems too many to count and numerous struggles to manage toward positive outcome with many failures and many successful transitions from problem to profit. In today's world you do not need to look far to find problems. To win you need to find them and confront them, see past the immediate and look to the future in how you can take the bad and move from bad to good. Sitting on the sideline makes for a long and boring game so get up and work hard so that you are able to produce results when the team needs you the most.

Famous people who do great and positive things do not accomplish deeds by sitting idle waiting for something to happen. A professional manager pushes and pulls; drags and lifts; runs and sprints; never gives up; and never stops. When the world runs out of problems and there is nothing more to do the professional manager may disappear, but until that happens what he/she does is important in the lives of many people and critical to the long-term success of the company or organization.

Ultimately it is the team that wins. As the leader of the team you want to be surrounded by people who will give it their best effort and can be counted on to do their jobs without prompting. It starts with recruiting and hiring the best people possible on your team. You can look for people in the same places as everyone else and end up hiring the same level of talent as everyone else, or you can set yourself apart from the rest and hire the best people available. Don't get caught in the trap of looking in the same place as all of the other recruiters. The quarterback can focus on the defensive set if he knows that the center will snap the ball correctly, the line will perform their blocking scheme, and the receivers will run the right patterns. A professional manager hires a winning team.

The interview process for most is a way of screening out applicants you do not want to hire leaving the final candidate who is by your best judgment, over a brief amount of time asking questions and listening to responses, the best of the bunch. Don't follow the rest of the pack with traditional interview questions. Use your managerial instinct and gut feel to guide you. You are a professional manager and you know how to read people. Find out what the candidate is really made of as a person and then, if your intuition tells you they are the right person, use the interview time to start leading the applicant toward your company and your department. Sell them on what you are doing and why it is a great opportunity for them. Hiring the best people takes more than just screening; it takes intuition, confidence, and salesmanship.

A big mistake that managers make is to move a person into the firing-line without the proper orientation and training and before they feel comfortable and confident in what they are doing. It is a sick feeling to be hired for a job and feel great about all the potential the manager sees in you and then all of a sudden, the manager disappears, and no one is showing you how to do the job. Demands from people come at you faster than you can respond, and you question whether you were hired for the same job that you applied for. Sometimes a new employee is left bored out of their mind because no one is showing them what to do. Remember you are a professional manager which means that the team members you employ will be given the attention they need from you to flourish. A good gardener knows that he/she cannot make flowers bloom immediately by tossing seeds on the ground and walking away. In order to have a spectacular garden he/she must plant, fertilize, cultivate, and water the plants with a nurturing spirit that brings them into full bloom and glory when the time is right.

Just as the professional athlete knows the team playbook well, the professional manager knows the company rules, regulations, policies and guidelines. Being in the wrong place, at the wrong time, doing the wrong thing will get a wide receiver in trouble and cause him to miss the block or pass. To execute to the best of his ability on every play he must study the playbook and follow the rules. The same is true for the professional manager. Holding the company or department playbook in high regard and becoming a student of the documents will help you maintain your edge in situations where you need to execute properly to stay on top of the game.

A well-organized manager maintains a filing system that makes it easy to keep track of employee performance and provides reference points that will help reinforce and recognize employees as well as identify areas for continued improvement. An employee will benefit from a professional manager's work to develop and improve their team members. A good coach has all the statistics on the team and on each player and studies the results. A great coach takes the information available and does something with it to make the team and players better.

Discipline is a means of maintaining good order and conduct in any group of people. Discipline also means that you as a manager act in a disciplined and appropriate manner. Your job as a professional manager is to use the disciplinary process to improve and correct employee behavior. Discipline is used to get rid of an undesirable employee only as a last resort and your intent to utilize discipline for this purpose should be minimal. A team without discipline is like a hole with no donut! What binds a team together is the discipline they all constitute and share with each other to excel and achieve. Some of the best teams have achieved success without a star player or stand-out performer. When all the starters and the bench are all performing well together at a high level it is hard for another team to beat them.

Positive reinforcement becomes your most influential tool for shaping and improving employee behavior. People want to receive recognition for the work they do. The reinforcement they seek should come from you as their manager. A professional manager looks for the good things that their employees do and takes the time to show their appreciation for a job well done. A professional manager knows his/her employees and cares about them as workers and as people. Sincerity and concern for the wellbeing of the team and team members comes naturally to the manager who is effective in an organization. A team that lacks recognition from the manager and players that do not recognize each other is like a pan of water that won't boil. It doesn't matter how much heat you apply to it the molecules won't interact with each other. A professional manager knows how important it is for all players to get recognized for their efforts and accomplishments. The leader of a winning team provides the atmosphere for all players to recognize each other and collectively accomplish more as a team.

In spite of everything that a professional manager does there will still be conflict. When more than one human is put into any situation the possibility of conflict exists. There is only one way to resolve conflict and that is to confront it head-on and work through it to permanent resolution. No one enjoys conflict and it is a normal manager's goal to minimize it as much as possible. A healthy environment embraces conflict for what it is without personalizing it. Searching for areas of potential conflict with the intent to bring those problems to the surface provides the professional manager a platform and springboard to stand on. Because there is a new problem to address the professional manager must use confrontation skills and achieve resolution. Sometimes a calm and smooth-running operation fails because without conflict there is no reason to change. With the need for change to reconcile and improve a situation basically the operation gets better and can move to a new level of efficiency. Remember, to a professional manager, problems beget profits, meaning we cannot improve the bottom-line unless we root out and exploit problems and drive new solutions for the business.

It does not matter whether the organization is small or massive, the personality types involved in the workgroup are critical to the entities' success. You as a manager must know the personality make-up of your teams and people and understand how different personality types respond to each other in the work environment. As a professional manager you will maintain a proper balance of various personality types in your work teams and will promote the understanding of the differences to everyone on the team. Why? Because not only do you need to know how to respond to and acknowledge a difference in perspective or thought pattern, you want your team to understand that difference is okay, and to respect and appreciate the differences in people. Why? Because an organization that looks outside the box sees things inside the box more clearly. People with different perspectives will provide unique and sometimes innovative ideas if they are allowed to, and as a result the organization becomes better.

Successfully managing conflict and difficult conversations becomes the norm for you as a professional manager just as a wide-receiver knows the pass pattern and runs it flawlessly so the quarterback can throw the ball before the receiver makes a cut inside to the point the ball is going to be caught. Executing on a play takes practice and experience to know how to respond to the situation and what skills will be needed to complete the play or work through the issue successfully. The relevance to personality types is intentional and critical to effective conflict resolution and successful conflict management. Why? Because the basics of creating win-win situations and the science behind confronting conflict is necessary to understand that in general terms all situations follow the prescribed paths based on how you as a manager approach the issue. When it comes to managing conflict from an employee's perspective it is important to learn more about how different people with different personality types will respond in a given situation. Active listening is critical to managing conflict. Being able to decipher the intent of the "sender" and also being able to anticipate and understand the impact of the "receiver" is important in conflict related discussions and dialogue. Here a manager is dealing with emotions and feelings, not logic and facts. Maintaining composure and balance is vital and the professional manager knows the importance of the phrase: "Emotions have no brains."

Successful communication occurs when the intended message is received by the intended target. In order for the message to be delivered successfully, the sender must take into account all of the biases and divergent paths that the information may travel so that it gets to the end point in the condition that it needs to be in to get the message across. How many times have you heard someone explain that there is a communication problem somewhere? When a problem arises, there is usually an element of communication that didn't occur, didn't get handled properly, or was mismanaged. Communication gets the blame for many failures in an organization whereas a more thorough investigation might reveal that the true collapse was with the manager's failure to properly assess the situation, understand or know what the correct message should be, or approach the situation with the professional manager's playbook wide open and applied appropriately. As a professional manager you are schooled in the art of communicating to a wide variety of people in a succinct and effective manner which allows you to get more done with less issues or problems.

The secret to motivating employees is your ability as a manager to create a positive work environment. A positive work environment is one that encourages people to motivate themselves to do a great job. Motivation is something that a person can do for themselves but is next to impossible for you to do for them. What you can do is reinforce behavior that supports your people's individual and collective actions toward positive improvement. When their work environment is positive, and they enjoy coming to work, employees are more productive. With a simple comment or action you can build up and reinforce a positive environment or tear it down – it doesn't take much to destroy it; it takes methodical and persistent action on the part of the manager to create and maintain the right work environment.

Managing people requires that you act responsibly. As a manager you expect your employees to also act responsibly. As a manager you cannot give responsibility to another person. You cannot delegate responsibility, nor can you force someone else to be responsible. Responsibility is very similar to motivation; it must come from within a person – it cannot be given to them. When the environment that the professional manager creates achieves a high level of respect for and sense of empowerment of the people on the team then the team performance improves. People prefer belonging to a team that provides them respect and empowers them to be responsible. For the vast majority of people this is true; for a few, managers will have to take a different approach. Too many managers spend too much time on the people that refuse to be responsible and end up showing less respect to the entire workgroup because of the emphasis on the few. When this happens over a long enough period of time the environment rots from within and becomes ineffective.

As you progress in your achievement of the professional manager level you continue to build your management credibility. As a professional manager you have never "Paid your dues" and therefore you cannot sit back and relax and expect everything you have built to stay intact. Maybe in other professions you can do this but as a manager you cannot. What it has taken years to build can slip away very quickly as the field you are playing in is constantly changing. Your playing field is the interactions and interpersonal relationships you have with people. People are always changing as they grow and develop. As a manager you will face new people at all levels of the organization. Credibility as a manager means you are always building something. You are always honing your basic management skills to strive to stay on top and keep your professional edge. A wide-receiver cannot afford to slack off in his training regiment or he will be beat by the defensive-back or miss the spot where he is to catch the ball. So it goes with the professional manager, always needing to stay in great managerial shape.

In the quest to find the idyllic manager there are certain things that the professional manager does very well, and you will notice these strengths and competencies if you are looking for them. Remember, the game is not about the coach, or the general manager, or the referee; it is about the players on the field. A great coach is not in the public eye attempting to get recognition; rather he/she is in the background working hard to get the team and the players all of the recognition they deserve for their work. A good referee is one who you will never remember or know because he/she does such a thorough and accurate job that the attention is on the game and not the penalty calls. The model manager has developed his/her rapport through formal means staying within the guidelines of being a professional manager. The model manager has also earned respect and power in the organization through informal means while staying within the guidelines of being a professional manager. Because he/she understands and works to develop the most productive and career satisfying department for his/her employees, the model manager attracts people who want to work in their organization and who, individually and collectively, continue to produce positive results.

Leadership can mean a lot of things in an organization. Effective leadership is what the professional manager strives for in everything they do. In order to be an effective leader, you must also be an effective follower who seeks to know and understand what your people need and tries to determine what they are capable of doing at any given point in time, as well as determining what they cannot do in a situation. Leading people down a trail or path requires walking in their shoes to see how they perceive what is happening to them. A great leader will know that at a certain point we need to stop and rest before taking on the next summit. By judging and moving with his/her people according to their needs and perceptions a leader can formulate a path that is achievable and build upon the confidence of the team to be able to do more. There are many leaders who push out ahead and drive their people forward not realizing that their people are not behind them. Physically they might be there but mentally they have checked-out. A professional manager always asks employees when directing them to do tasks and never presents a request as a demand that they do something. A professional manager wants people to want to follow them and do the things that they are asked to do, otherwise a manager should not want their employees to feel like they are doing things begrudgingly because they have been ordered to do something.

Your goal as a professional manager will always be to build a supportive climate for the team. Key factors to keep in mind to build a supportive climate are open communication, being accessible to your people, and engaging people in the business. Your success as a manager is predicated on your employee's success. The more that they are engaged in the decision-making process and the more that they contribute to the strategy for the department or business, the more acceptance and forward progress will occur. Working through your employees you will achieve more! Seems simple but so many managers work around employees, do things in-spite of their employees, whine and complain about what they can't do because of their employees, etc. All these signs are indications of a managerial breakdown in the process of building a supportive climate. If there are barriers to productivity in the work environment keeping yourself and your team from performing, remove them. If you have an employee-centered focus you will see the barriers and opportunities at ground level and if you engage your people in the process, following the guidelines established in the professional manager's playbook, you will always get positive results.

The whole purpose for the organization is to satisfy a business or market need. Meeting customer needs becomes vital to the existence of the organization. A chapter on this subject is included in the professional manager's playbook because it is very important people understand how customers react to the service they receive. Positioning your department as a small business servicing the needs of internal and external customers helps your team think through the impact of the actions they take in performing their daily work. If every employee completed each day thinking through what dollar value they brought to the bottom-line that day and how that improvement in cost or revenue supported their salary and the benefits they receive, the activities that employees engage in would be better aligned with behaviors that drive monetary improvements to the business. There are connections to every possible position within a company to the end customer. Help your employees think through things from a customer's perspective and ask themselves "if I were the customer would I have written a check to pay for the work that was completed today?" Aligning employees with the bottom-line and what the customers would be willing to pay for is a way of grounding your people and sailing the business through profitable waters.

Another perspective is to help your team see that for internal customers, they have other options. If you don't provide the support that internal customers need to get their jobs done efficiently, they will find alternative ways of getting what they need; this may mean not using your department. This does not bode well for you and your team in the long-run. As a small business within the organization you want to see your team grow, develop, and prosper.

Employee evaluation and development keeps the employee management machine running. The best employees you will lose will be lost due to your involvement in developing them and promoting them. Identifying areas to focus for developing an employee skill set, drawing out a hidden strength buried inside an employee, or bringing visibility and polish to an employee by promoting an existing strength is a gratifying experience for the professional manager. A caution in employee evaluation and development is that as a manager you do not try to be the expert on everything. No one person can possibly be an expert at everything. We want to promote and develop our people in everything we can to make sure we have a strong and balanced team; that includes you as a manager. Knowing and living the basics about employee management in this playbook will give you all the expertise you need to be a successful and professional manager.

Remember no matter how good the team is that you are playing on, no matter how skilled the coach or your manager is at managing people, no matter how cooperative or experienced your peers are, and no matter whether the business is stagnant, failing, or growing like crazy, the one thing you can control is you. You are a professional manager, don't forget that, so stay focused on your skill development and keep your managerial muscles in shape. You will be known for who you are and what you have done to manage people well, known as a great boss and a great leader. These are the most important statistics in the game, not that you played for a certain team or you had a specific title; rather that you are a well respected and professional manager known for who he/she is as a person.

Acknowledgements

The author wishes to acknowledge the assistance of several individuals in the creation of this book. First and foremost, for all of the managers I have worked for that have helped me along my path in management. For Tom who took a chance on me and hired me to get it all started. For his mentoring and assistance in spite of the short time he had on this earth; I know you are looking down from above and helping me!

For my wife and our children who provide acceptance and insight and support my work, the love and support you give me helps me keep the pen to the paper and the drive to find answers in support of my family. For our son David who is with us in spirit, guiding and moving my fingers across the keyboard, I would not be able to do what I do without your spirit in my life.

For my mother (who guides me now in spirit) who is the best editor and supporter of my work, who never missed a punctuation, spelling, or grammatical error, I greatly appreciate your time, energy and support of my work.

I thank all of you and I love you.

Bibliography

Performance Management: Improving Quality and Productivity through Positive Reinforcement, Aubrey C. Daniels, Ph.D., Theodore A. Rosen, Ph.D., Performance Management Publications, Inc. Tucker, GA, Second Edition, 1984

Difficult Conversations: How to Discuss What Matters Most, Stone, Patton, Heen, Viking Press, 1999

Difficult Conversations: Successfully Managing Conflict, dor and associates, Minneapolis, MN, 2003

Documenting Performance Issues – A Road Map for Employee Success, Mike Deblieux Human Resources, 1999

Presenting With Impact, Personnel Decisions International Corporation, 2003

About the Author

Rory Evans Wilson graduated from Drake University with a Bachelor of Science degree, major in Human Resource Management with extensive work in psychology, sociology, religion, and history. In addition to this book on managerial development, Wilson writes spiritual non-fiction, poetry, historical fiction and also lyrics and music. In addition to his career in distribution management, he is actively involved in youth activities and teen ministry. Wilson and his wife coordinate fundraising events to support charities which contribute money to children in need both in the United States and around the world. He and his family live in the Midwest.